ABOUT TH

Emma De Vita is features e   _anagement Today_. During
her years on the magazine, s.   .ias spent time in jail, watching
catwalk shows and travelling to São Paolo, New York
and Mumbai all in the name of business journalism, for
which she has won a number of awards. Her articles have
also appeared in the _Sunday Times_, the _Guardian_ and the
Financial Times.

'A very practical, colourful and readable leadership toolkit
that draws on the wisdom of those in the know to provide a
useful compendium of clear analysis and ideas.'
        Cilla Snowball, group CEO and chairman, AMV.BBDO

'Holistic leadership, both on an individual and on a corporate
level, offers one of the greatest opportunities to business today.
This book makes an important contribution by helping its
readers identify and develop their own capability, and grow as
authentic and inspiring leaders.'
        Paul Walsh, CEO, Diageo

THE LEADERSHIP
MASTERCLASS

Great business ideas without the hype

management today

not just business as usual

THE LEADERSHIP
MASTERCLASS

Great business ideas without the hype

Edited by Emma De Vita

headline

business plus

First published in 2010 by
HEADLINE PUBLISHING GROUP

1

Cataloguing in Publication Data is available from the British Library

ISBN 978 0 7553 6015 4

Typeset in Bembo and Avenir by Susie Bell, www.f-12.co.uk

Printed and bound in the UK by
CPI Mackays, Chatham ME5 8TD

HEADLINE PUBLISHING GROUP
An Hachette UK Company
338 Euston Road
London NW1 3BH

www.headline.co.uk
www.hachette.co.uk

CONTENTS

ACKNOWLEDGEMENTS

Thanks to all *Management Today* contributors, past and present. With particular thanks to Octavius Black and The Mind Gym for 'Your Route to the Top', Alexander Garrett for 'Crash Course', Helen Kirwan-Taylor for 'Are You Suffering From', John Morrish for 'Words-Worth', Stefan Stern for 'Masterclass', Jennifer Harris for 'Why Business is Like', and Andrew Saunders, Hannah Prevett, James Taylor and David Waller for their own contributions.

Thanks also to Professor Rob Goffee and Professor Gareth Jones for permission to use an extract from 'Lead Your Way', which featured in the February 2006 issue of *MT*, based on their book *Why Should Anyone Be Led by You?* (Harvard Business Press, 2006). Also thanks to Patrick Esson, MD of Aransa, which provides services to improve the way people negotiate and make decisions. He contributed 'the keys to building and maintaining trust' on pages 34-5.

With special thanks to John Moseley for his encouragement, for Robert Kirby and to Matthew Gwyther for their support. A thank you to Simon Lees and the rest of the *MT* team.

Finally, to Simon and my parents.

FOREWORD

The first thing that anyone will tell you about leadership is that it's very personal.

Quite right: being a leader comes from an awareness of who you are and what you stand for - and staying true to that. You can't borrow authenticity from someone else.

So this book doesn't try to give you a rigid leadership model to follow. Instead, it offers straightforward advice on the things you need to think about as you find your own way.

Of course, the subject of leadership is not exclusively for those at the very top of an organisation. In today's workplace, with its flat and flexible structures, leaders no longer sit at the top of a pyramid handing down decisions. At Sky, as in many other organisations, leaders are everywhere.

And so, one of my top priorities as a chief executive is to nurture and develop those leaders today, and to make them increasingly capable for the future. After all, they are the people who will, I hope, lead my organisation to success long after I have left.

That leadership potential is crucial because Sky is, at its heart, a business of people and ideas. Technology may become obsolete. TV programmes may go out of fashion. If they do, I'm confident we'll be able to adapt and renew. But if we don't have the right people and the right leaders in the business, then we will fail. They are the only sustainable source of success.

So, while there is no unique template for good leadership, I spend a lot of time thinking about what our future leaders will look like.

What they will not be, in my view, is narrowly defined by their technical skills or professional qualifications. In a fast-changing world, the shelf life of those skills has already shortened and will only shorten further in the future. To be successful, tomorrow's leaders will need to be far more rounded individuals than ever before. For me, five traits stand out.

Top of the list is the ability and, indeed, the desire to collaborate in pursuit of shared goals. I think of that as the first step on the ladder of leadership.

Beyond that, I'm looking for an ability to set clear direction and make things happen. In short, the ability to turn activity into results.

He or she must have a desire to support and coach others so that they too can give their best and fulfil their own potential. That means guiding, challenging and supporting, not dictating from above.

I want to see an understanding that perpetual improvement is the basis for future success. Leaders have an ethos of learning and development, for themselves and the people they lead, that stays with them throughout their career.

And finally, in a world where change has become the new status quo, I'm looking for people who embrace change, rather than resist it; leaders who have a bias for action, combined with an ability to learn from their mistakes.

These are the people who will succeed at Sky. But Sky is not unique in this respect. I believe leaders who display these traits can be successful anywhere. That's the point about leadership. It is critical to all organisations. Those who hone and develop their leadership skills will achieve lasting success for themselves and the organisations in which they work.

Jeremy Darroch, chief executive, BSkyB

INTRODUCTION

This book is for anyone with an appetite for leadership. You may just be starting out in your career, striving for your first leadership position or be a *bona fide* leader a few years into the job. Engaged in your work and wanting to get ahead? This book will give you the leadership leg-up that you need. It's for those in large corporations, entrepreneurs at the helm of growing businesses, as well as those in the public and charity sectors.

Serving as a companion to *The Management Masterclass*, *The Leadership Masterclass* builds on the essential skills that you learnt in the first book but takes you to the next career stage. *Management Today* may be the UK's leading monthly business magazine but it isn't just about 'business as usual'. We pride ourselves in giving you practical, no-nonsense words of wisdom from those who have actually been there and done it. So, if you need advice on becoming the best, no matter where you are on the career ladder, then we've got it covered.

This second book draws on some of the best advice that we've given our readers, as well as providing some brand new ideas. The emphasis is on giving you leadership inspiration based on real life rather than a prescriptive, business-school model that urges you to follow a specific path. It's about alerting you to the things that matter but then leaving you to devise your own leadership style that allows you to achieve your best.

Leadership has been a fashionable favourite among business thinkers ever since they started thinking about business. It's unfortunate that many now regard it as something distinct and somehow superior to management, because the two cross over considerably. Every manager has to be a leader in some capacity, anyone in fact where someone else looks to you for direction. You could be a teacher, a small-business owner or a middle manager in a bank.

Yet, it must be recognised that it does take a certain type of person to hanker after and go for the top job. Those possessed with the vocation to lead sometimes make poor managers – the two don't go hand in hand. And it takes all sorts to make a successful leader. Enlightened leadership is about allowing people to create their own distinctive style, and not emulate a perceived ideal. Much has been written, for example, about the different styles of different generations (generation X versus generation Y), and of how men and women behave. So, while a male boss in his sixties might expect adherence to a strict hierarchy, a young female leader in her thirties might prefer a more collaborative, flexible approach to leadership. Both approaches are equally acceptable and can be very successful.

And, just like the world of couture, fashions within the discipline of leadership come and go, reflecting the particular zeitgeist. A great deal has changed since *Management Today* first started writing about leadership in the 1960s. Take, for example, a 1967 survey of 102 company directors, which revealed an average age of 56, 71 per cent of whom were public-school educated, with 32 per cent having gone to Oxbridge. In such a clubbable world, there was no need to ask if any of them were women. These days, leaders tend to come from more diverse backgrounds and be younger in age. The changed demographic of those in the very senior echelons of business has an influence that seeps down through an organisation, encouraging greater diversity – and different ways of thinking – that benefit businesses in a globalised and high-tech world.

The 1970s was a gloomy time for leaders. Petrol queues, striking dustmen and recession weighed heavy on business. Some parallels could be drawn with today's economic situation but when it comes to work and leadership, there are definitely some all too familiar similarities. In 1976, *Management Today* offered some examples of bad-boss behaviour that still (unfortunately) ring true today. Recognise any of the following? 'He is never available', 'he keeps changing his mind', and, of course, that perennial favourite, 'he takes all the credit'.

The 1980s brought a leader of a different kind – Margaret Thatcher. At first, *Management Today* wondered where she was leading UK business but we soon sensed good times for managers. But it wasn't until 1986, with the long-awaited computerisation and deregulation of the London Stock Exchange (aka the Big Bang), that the British approach to business fundamentally changed. The rise of the Square Mile was rapid, and along with it came the ripping up of the rule book.

The past two decades brought huge cultural changes, including the development of the internet, the mass entry (at last!) of women into managerial and leadership positions, and the globalisation of business. So, where do leaders find themselves in the 2010s? Under pressure, more than at any other recent time. The emphasis now is on transparency, trustworthiness and ingenuity. Leadership these days – unlike the 1960s when 'command and control' was favoured – is about being authentic and working smartly.

More than ever before, being a leader in the twenty-first century is also about working collaboratively – just think of the coalition government created in the UK in the wake of the 2010 General Election. Being able to share power and still maintain a sense of momentum and authority while getting decisions made quickly is a rare but incredibly important skill to possess.

But the biggest leadership problem that remains is getting more women into the upper echelons of business and the public sector. It's a challenge that has reached critical proportions, and despite all the research and the good intentions, it's a problem that just won't go away. All that's known for sure is that it can't be allowed to go on for much longer. So take some time to think what it is you can do about it ...

If you read this book from cover to cover then we hope you'll learn something useful for every aspect of your job. If on the other hand it just sits on your desk to provide emergency advice and inspiration during tricky situations, then we hope we can get you out of your scrape. The aim is to give you a masterclass in leadership that will become your career companion.

The book is divided into five chapters. The first chapter – **What is Your Style?** – asks you to explore what kind of leader you want to be. What are your unique strengths, and how can you use them to create a distinct leadership style that will set you on a course for success? Being a brilliant twenty-first century leader is also about instilling the right values and culture in the team you lead, whether it's two people or an entire organisation.

The second chapter – **To Boldly Go...** – is about how to behave as a leader, giving you advice on what you should and shouldn't be doing during your early days as a leader, to the things to consider once you've settled in. It gives guidance on a range of common and less common problems, from acquiring gravitas to controlling your ego (should it exceed suitable limits). It's one thing to be confident; another to be arrogant. As we point out, the best leaders are the ones that have a degree of humility.

The third chapter is about **Strategy**, from the basics to the extras. Strategy is primarily a leadership concern, but devising one is not the same as being a manager and executing one. Learn what an 'emotionally intelligent strategy', an 'adhocracy' and a 'silo' are. The fourth chapter – **Reputation** – is a peculiarly twenty-first-century leadership concern. It's not only about how to create a personal reputation that is the envy of your rivals, but it's also about establishing and maintaining a brilliant reputation for your organisation.

The final chapter – **Lessons from the Top** – steers away from theory and presents instead the wisest words from the good and the great of business and beyond. This is where we present our 'Lessons from the Top' from the people who have actually sat in the hot seat, be it Archie Norman, the late Sir John Harvey-Jones, James Murdoch or Stevie Smith. What career lessons have they picked up on the way to the top, and what would they do differently if they had to start all over again?

What's striking is just how unplanned many successful careers have been. The common thread is having a passion for whatever it is they are doing, and having the flexibility and nous to spot an opportunity and go for it. Because, at the end of the day, what's the point in making all the sacrifices that come with being a leader, if you don't enjoy what you do?

Emma De Vita
July 2010

WHAT IS YOUR STYLE?

'Everybody loves success but they hate successful people'
JOHN McENROE SAID IT

Congratulations. You've made it into the metaphorical corner office – you're the head honcho now. Or maybe you've been boss for a while but you're still feeling a little bit like an imposter… Yes, they gave you the job; you won the promotion but you're still feeling a little unconfident about things. What exactly are leaders meant to do after all? And why hasn't anyone told you how to do it?

Relax. You're not the only one to feel this way. In fact, if you felt you were master or mistress of the universe a week into the leader's job, then we'd have to say the person who hired you has made a mistake. Arrogance isn't an attractive trait for any leader. Actually, there are no exact rules to guide you into becoming an excellent boss. Most successful CEOs or MDs develop their approach to leading over time, following hunches, learning from mistakes and taking risks. If they're lucky, they have a handful of mentors they can call on when they need to. So, it's important that you cultivate a network of trusted advisers that you can rely on for support and encouragement. Remember, it can get lonely at the top sometimes.

You've got this far already so you've clearly got what it takes to be a great leader. But now it's time to give the nature of leadership – and what it means to you personally – a little more thought. What is different about you that equips you to lead? Or to put it another way, what is it about yourself that inspires others to follow? Is it your confidence? Your determination? Your flair for problem solving? Or is it your relaxed manner? How do you like to think of yourself? Are you a maverick leader, a genius or something altogether different?

THE LEADERSHIP MASTERCLASS

WORDS-WORTH:
MAVERICK

A 'maverick' is an independent-minded outsider, a non-conformist, a rugged individualist. Think Michael O'Leary, John Madejski, Stelios Haji-Ioannou or Tom Cruise in Top Gun. The word is redolent of the American frontier, not least because it was the title of a 1950s TV series, with James Garner as Bret Maverick, a gambler and adventurer roaming the Old West. But its use to describe a person of unorthodox views is older, first recorded in 1880 in the Galveston (Texas) Daily News, which referred to 'political mavericks'. It was a metaphor: a maverick was an unbranded calf, wandering loose on the range. Here's one explanation: Samuel A. Maverick was a wealthy Texas politician and landowner who once acquired 400 cattle in settlement of a debt. He left the herd in another family's care, but it was neglected, and soon unbranded calves escaped. Men were sent out to look for these cattle, described first as 'Maverick's', and later as 'mavericks', to stop other people claiming them. It is entirely coincidental that some 'mavericks' speak a lot of bull.

Or maybe you fancy yourself as a bit of a genius?

WORDS-WORTH:
GENIUS

What could be nicer than to call someone a 'genius'? Regular nominees include Jack Welch, Rupert Murdoch, Bill Gates – and the man who invented Big Brother. In pagan times, your 'genius' was the spirit that oversaw your whole life. Later, it meant your general disposition. Only since the nineteenth century has it been possible to be 'a genius', someone with extraordinary, semi-divine powers. Those abilities – usually contrasted with mere 'talent' – are handy in business. They are also, strictly speaking, innate; but that hasn't stopped entrepreneurial types offering to make you a genius through books and seminars. That's perhaps because genius today has real commercial value. Where would the Virgin brand be without its peculiar 'genius'? And what about Steve Jobs, whose aura of omniscient cool saved Apple when it had gone rotten? In his booming high-street stores you can queue at the 'Genius Bar' and have your computer questions answered by semi-divine youths with 'Genius' for their job description.

Knowing yourself is the first step to becoming a leader, but you must also act as a leader. In their book *Why Should Anyone Be Led by You?*, London Business School professor Rob Goffee and consultant Gareth Jones argue that leadership is a relationship, and that a leader's skill in managing relationships, communicating inspirationally and with good timing, is critical. They write that: 'Good leaders manage relationships by knowing when to be close – to empathise, to build relations of warmth, loyalty and affection; and when to be distant – to keep people focused on the goal, to address poor performance, to give relationships an edge.' They suggest that all leaders ask the following key questions:

1   Which personal differences could form the basis of your leadership capability? Which of your characteristics have the potential to excite others; are genuinely yours; signify something important in your context? Think, too, about your personal values and vision for those you are leading.

2   Are you able to read different contexts? How well are you able to pick up on subtle shifts in the behaviour of others? Are you equally adept with bosses, peers and subordinates? What about customers and competitors? With those you like as well as dislike? How do you adapt across cultures? Are you better one-to-one, in a small group or with large gatherings?

3   Do you conform enough? Can you recognise the moment to hold back? Can you gain acceptance with others, without losing your authenticity?

4   How well do you manage social distance? Are you able to get close to those you lead? Do you know the goals and motives of those who have the biggest impact on your performance? What do you need to know more about? Are you able to separate and create distance from others – at the right moment?

Reprinted with permission from *Why Should Anyone Be Led by You? What It Takes to Be an Authentic Leader* by Rob Goffee and Gareth Jones. Harvard Business Press, 2006

You must be doing something right to have got this far – there's something about you that has convinced others that you've got what it takes to create followers. It's what you do to build on this that will make you stand out from the others. You have to develop a leadership style that you're comfortable with, that's convincing to those you lead and manage, and that will get you the best results. It's also about setting the right example.

'Setting an example is not the main means of influencing another, it is the only means'
ALBERT EINSTEIN SAID IT

CRASH COURSE IN...
LEADING BY EXAMPLE

You don't have a choice. From the moment you take up a leadership role, people will be watching you, so you are leading by example; the question is whether it's the example you want to set.

Be strategic. Identify the behaviours you want people to emulate. Some of these are driven by your organisation's values, others by the business context. If you ask your people to work unpaid, they'll expect to see that this is consistent with a broader business strategy and not a fad. They need to see a rationale, and that this isn't just a heroic gesture.

Walk the talk. Leading by example means you don't ask others to do what you are not prepared to do yourself. The whole idea is heavily linked to integrity, and people's antennae are tuned to hypocrisy right now.

Be aware of symbolism. Don't invest in a slew of new cars for senior management when you've just made people redundant, for example.

Show your tough side. It's not all about self-sacrifice. Giving tough feedback to people who are not performing – in a developmental way – may be the behaviour you want people to emulate.

Be visible. Leaders need to lead. It's not enough to retreat to the boardroom and tell people what you want them to do. You need to meet people face to face, rather than avoiding anxiety-provoking situations.

Validate. Check that the example people are digesting is the one you intended. Cultural surveys and 360-degree appraisals can help secure this feedback. It's not a quick fix; people will watch over an extended period to see how congruent your actions are. The best way to find out what people are really thinking is to talk to them.

Broaden your audience. The example you set through leadership should be aimed at external audiences as well as your own people.

Do say: 'The leadership that we show now during hard times will be remembered for years to come.'

Don't say: 'I'm going to be holidaying in Tuscany instead of the Caribbean this year, and I expect you all to do the same.'

VALUES

Your leadership foundations are your guiding principles, values and ethos. These will hold you in good stead as a first-class leader and will be mirrored in the culture you establish in your team, department or organisation. Your leadership values should complement those of your organisation, and vice versa.

WORDS-WORTH:
VALUES

Businesses have always been about value. Now they are also expected to have 'values'. These are guiding principles, usually expressed through sanctimonious platitudes on motivational posters and corporate websites, where they mostly go unnoticed. Making the world a more beautiful place is tricky when you also have a business to run. Striving for uplift, it can be hard to strike the right note, especially since 'I have a dream' has already been taken. 'We continually seek to offer more for less,' promises one recruitment company. 'We all understand that sometimes we won't get there but often we shall achieve spectacular success,' boasts a banana importer. 'We like you just the way you are,' simpers The Body Shop. A 1920s coining, first used in sociology, 'values' are the things you value: the beliefs a person or society lives by. 'Values' really require a soul, but that will be a tall order for most companies.

History lessons: Walk the talk

When Anita Roddick founded The Body Shop in 1976, ethics was something to trouble philosophy students, not bosses of big business. Thirty-five years on, however, the corporate world has caught on: ethics sells. Tesco, Asda and M&S are among retailers looking to convince us of their purist creed. Even energy giants like Shell, long in the crosshairs of green campaigners, have run ads showing flowers floating dreamily out of factory smokestacks. Trouble is, you have to mean it. Roddick breathed ethics, pioneering audits of suppliers and campaigning for human rights. She always nailed her colours to the mast: a fine example to modern chief execs.

It's true to say that some of the most successful leaders impress others not by their super-high levels of confidence or their terrifying presence, but by their humility. They never assume they know best – in fact, they always ask others for their opinion, and listen to them when they give it. Make sure you include being humble in your leadership style: it's a necessary value.

YOUR ROUTE TO THE TOP...
HOW TO BE HUMBLE

Open up. Get the most out of your team by welcoming their views. Appreciate everyone's contribution and you'll create more innovative solutions, together.

Go for gold, not glory. Author Jim Collins compared the performance of high-profile CEOs with those who stay out of the limelight, and found that it's results, not status, that count. Focus on your role, not your profile.

Don't tell, show. You don't have to be full of charisma, but simply demonstrate the high standards you expect. Inspiring behaviour can be more powerful than an inspiring speech.

Let others shine. Deflect discussions about yourself by praising the contributions of others. Lou Gerstner, who stopped IBM from crumbling in the 1990s, illustrates this: 'Change came to IBM in large part due to the pride and energy of the employees themselves ... My role was to kick-start the process.'

Have faith. Coleman Mockler turned Gillette around, and retained remarkable balance in his work and home life – even during the darkest times of takeover crisis. His secret?

Trusting the team that he'd assembled. Cultivate a team of experts and they'll build greatness, even when you're not there.

Selectively reveal weaknesses. Let people see that you're human and they'll feel comfortable working on their own weaknesses. Don't gloss over imperfections and you'll motivate others to get to where you are now.

Ask for feedback. No one operates in isolation, so it's important to ask for regular and continuous feedback. If you're brave enough, then instituting a 360° feedback policy will tell you everything you need to know.

Step back. Create something that will live on, long after you've moved on. One humble CEO said: 'I want to look from my porch, see the company as one of the great companies in the world, and be able to say: "I used to work there."'

You can't be any kind of leader if your followers don't trust you. As soon as trust disappears, you can wave goodbye to your reputation, your efficacy – and even your job. Trust adds great value to an organisation by strengthening relationships, boosting morale and improving productivity. It demands both character and competence. A competent, dishonest person is obviously not trustworthy. But an incompetent person, however well intentioned, can't be trusted either. Trust takes time to grow, but can be destroyed in an instant. So, what are the keys to building and maintaining trust?

1 Establish consistent values. Promote core values that are consistent with each other and with factors critical to the success of the organisation. There's no point stressing quality as a value, if success relies on being cheap, or valuing initiative, if compliance is crucial.

2 Lead by example. Embody the core values. Leaders must establish what is paramount and walk the talk with conviction. Nothing undermines trust as quickly as saying one thing and doing another.

3 Share a credible plan. People need confidence in their leaders' ability to achieve their goals. Let people know what is going on, see that there is a sound plan, and feel that they have an important part to play in it. Don't imply it's not their concern.

4 Delegate wisely. Delegate the task, not the method. Make sure people know what's needed and ensure they have the right skills, tools and resources. Don't blame others if you delegate badly.

5 Empower people by coaching. Encourage people to think for themselves. Coach those who need some guidance. It will help them grow in confidence and reassure you of their ability. Don't micro-manage – that achieves the very opposite of building trust.

6 Develop reliability. Don't promise things you can't deliver. Always follow through on things you say you will do. Insist others do the same. If, for some reason, it becomes impossible to honour a previous commitment, tell those affected as soon as possible. Don't surprise them at the last minute and leave them to pick up the pieces. To ensure others do the same, don't punish their honesty.

7 Have trust as your default. Trust people unless you have good reason not to but don't be reckless (see 4

and 5). When you trust people, their self-respect grows and they will not want to let you down. If you treat them with suspicion, they will resent it, lose confidence in their own ability and then let you down.

8 Tolerate mistakes. Admit your own mistakes and embolden others to do the same. Don't stigmatise them. Remember the old adage: nothing ventured, nothing gained. Trying to eliminate the possibility of mistakes shows a lack of trust. Learn from mistakes, then forgive them.

9 Improve two-way communication. Tell the truth. People hate being in the dark. Silence breeds uncertainty, doubt and worry. It implies lack of concern, lack of respect and lack of trust. Why should people be denied the truth or the courtesy of regular updates? Be humble and respect the opinion and interests of others. Encourage people to express opinions openly, provide honest feedback and share new ideas.

10 Foster loyalty. Be loyal up, down and sideways – and expect the same from others. Don't pass the buck when things go wrong. Know what matters to those you lead, stand up for them, protect their welfare, and secure the best possible conditions for them. Express your views clearly before a decision is made, but once it's taken, support it fully. Reject criticism and gossip, especially casual sniping on social media networks like Twitter and Facebook. Heed the advice of management thinker Steven Covey: one of the most important ways to manifest integrity is to be loyal to those who are not present. In doing so, we build the trust of those who are present. Finally, remember, this is not a pick and mix. Complete integrity requires all ten.

If trust is the first musketeer, then transparency is the second, and accountability is the third – one for all, and all for one!

WORDS-WORTH:
TRANSPARENCY

'Transparency' is one of the great business mantras of our day. To be transparent is to be open, accountable, honest. You need to display transparency in your dealings with colleagues, suppliers and customers. Transparency is the opposite of secrecy. In leadership, it means not only informing people of your decisions, but allowing them to see the process by which you arrived at them. It's a lot to ask. The word comes from the Latin preposition trans– *meaning 'across' and the verb* parare, *meaning 'to appear', or 'be visible'. It was first used here in English in the fifteenth century, in its literal sense. The figurative sense, meaning open in behaviour, is first recorded in Shakespeare. The business use seems to have taken off in the latter years of the twentieth century. It is worth noting that the international anti-corruption organisation Transparency International was founded in 1993: it is said that 'not transparent' is diplomatic language for 'corrupt'. Transparency, then, is a good thing. And yet, if you call a person 'transparent', it is not a compliment. 'You're so transparent,' you say, meaning that person's bad intentions, though not expressed, are obvious. That's the thing about transparency: you can't only look good, you have to be good. A lot to ask, indeed.*

Masterclass in Accountability:
What is it?

US President Harry S. Truman understood accountability. 'The buck stops here' read the little sign on his desk. He was answerable for the actions of his government and his country. Managers need to know to whom they must answer, be it shareholders, the board or trustees. Proponents of corporate social responsibility (CSR) argue that organisations have many stakeholders to whom bosses are accountable. The risk of being so to everybody for everything, however, is that you can forget about the grubby business of making money. And if lines of accountability are not clear, no one is accountable at all.

Where did it come from?

At first, businesses were run by their owners, with family firms establishing dynasties. But as they grew larger, the concept of the professional manager emerged: a hired hand accountable to owners, operating on their behalf. Michael Jensen's 'agency theory' suggests that managers' interests have to be aligned with those of the owners – i.e., shareholders – through, say, share options. The consequence of this has been to encourage managers to manipulate share prices over the short term, to the long-term detriment of shareholders. Now, the concept gets more confusing. John Sunderland, the ex-CEO of Cadbury, said that the owners towards whom he wanted to be accountable were more elusive, less predictable and less communicative than in the past. The very word 'ownership' is ceasing to describe the relationship between the company and its investors. Owners – hedge funds, private equity and the like – are getting harder to recognise. The (share) price mechanism risks becoming the only serious discipline being exerted on management.

So, you've identified your defining leadership qualities, worked on developing these into your own distinctive style, and settled on the values you wish to live by (and have others in your organisation follow). Now you have to weave these different strands together to create a distinctive organisational culture...

CULTURE

'The attainment of an ideal is often the beginning of disillusion'
STANLEY BALDWIN SAID IT

It's always good to have a vision and to aim high. But in truth, reality never lives up to expectations and you have to be prepared for this – don't get committed to an unachievable ideal. And don't fall into the trap of wanting to make your mark by getting rid of everything that went before you. On the other hand, you have got the freedom and the power to change things – you don't just have to conform to what went before.

'Conformity is the jailer of freedom and the enemy of growth'
JOHN F. KENNEDY SAID IT

Masterclass in Having a Vision:
What is it?

Even before he was voted out of office in 1992, President Bush Snr knew he had a problem with what he called 'the vision thing'. A vision is what an inspiring leader or organisation has: a view of the world, its place in it and an idea of what it wants to achieve. Business guru Warren Bennis says leaders need a vision that others can believe in and come to adopt themselves. That is how to command attention. In a world of blind organisations, the ones with vision rule.

Where did it come from?

People have been having visions since biblical times. The Good Book says: 'Where there is no vision, the people perish.' Ever since, 'lonely leaders' have required a vision with which to inspire their followers. There are dangers in this, of course. Hitler had a vision of a 1,000-year Reich. It brought his country and half the planet to its knees. By contrast, Martin Luther King had a vision that still inspires today. But the fine talk can delay action. As Lou Gertsner said when he took over at IBM in 1993: 'The last thing this company needs right now is a vision.' And yet, secretly, he had one: survival. In *Built to Last*, Jerry Porras and Jim Collins say that a well-conceived vision has two main components: a core ideology and an envisioned future. Such a vision builds on 'what we stand for' (and won't change), and sets out 'what we seek to achieve' (which will require change and adaptation). Their entire work (and Collins's subsequent *Good to Great*) focuses on what they call successful 'visionary companies'. So the message is: get a vision, fast, that inspires your people to perform, while remembering the danger in setting up ludicrous goals that won't be believed. As one manager at a multinational commented recently: 'In this company we don't have a vision, we have a hallucination.'

One unique benefit about being a leader of an organisation (or a department or a team) is that you have a big-picture view of it while being in a position to change things – something no one else has.

WORDS-WORTH:
HELICOPTER VIEW

To take a 'helicopter view' is, as the name suggests, to rise above the detail of a situation and look at the big picture. It is, literally, an overview. It's a piece of contemporary jargon, but older than you might think. Its original source seems to be the real 'helicopter views' that feature on television news in America, where police-car chases provide a regular part of the programming. The earliest published example of the phrase being used in the modern sense was in the New York Times *in 1981, in an article about a famous architect accused of taking 'a helicopter view' of housing, after building an estate of new homes without consulting any of its likely residents. That's the kind of mistake you are liable to make if you look at everything from up in the sky and never from ground level: not for nothing is the 'helicopter view' also known as the '10,000 ft view'. The air is clear up there, but sooner or later you have to come down. Happy landings!*

YOUR ROUTE TO THE TOP...
HOW TO CREATE A VISION/MISSION

Inspire your people with a vision (what we want to achieve) or mission (what we are here to do). Targets may motivate but rarely produce the zest and determination that brings about extraordinary performance.

Make your mission powerful. Inspirational visions may be about revolution (shaking up the monoliths in your industry) or doing something worthwhile (making people's dreams come true).

Make the vision bold. Great visions can be impossible to achieve: 'Within an arm's reach of desire' (Coca-Cola); 'A computer on every desk and in every home' (Microsoft). Better resonant and bold than realistic.

Use your vision/mission as a touchstone. If an option or decision doesn't help the vision, don't follow it.

Be single-minded. Your vision should not be up for debate. This will demonstrate determination and passion and provide a clear focus to rally disparate employees.

Give each team its own mission consistent with the company aim but a lot more specific – e.g., 'removing waste so we can invest in the future' or 'helping our customers feel good about their decisions'.

Involve colleagues in developing the vision. Make sure they raise their sights above 'being number one in our chosen markets'. Instead, ask: 'Will this mission make me keen to jump out of bed on a rainy Monday morning in two years' time?'

Create a tale about your business's future. Imagining what clients, competitors, graduates and gurus will be thinking about you in five years will help the vision come to life. Include criticisms to give credibility.

Make sure your vision makes sound business sense rather than the result of excessive away-day exuberance before you go public. A vision is a communication tool, not a strategic management quick-fix.

You may have a vision – an idea even of how you want to change things – but you're not going to get anywhere on your own. Leaders may complain that it's lonely at the top but you never work in isolation. The best leaders are those who have a trusted team of people around them, whose skills complement their own.

History lessons: NASA

The launch of Sputnik 1 in 1957 gave the US the willies. Would the ominous bleeping ball orbiting above its citizens lead to atomic bombs from space? Faced with rising public hysteria, President Eisenhower convened NASA, assembling a team of galacticos equal to the apocalyptic technical challenge. Backroom boffins included Wernher von Braun, brain behind the Nazis' V-2 rocket, but less controversial talent covered the scientific spectrum. Four months after Sputnik, the US had a satellite in space. But the battle wasn't just scientific: the US needed heroes. Downhome Presbyterian John Glenn set the tone, with his pronouncement that his flight would 'take me closer to God'. His fellow astronauts Alan Shepard and Scott Carpenter were soon lionised as selfless patriots too. The nation wept tears of joy with every mission. Having set its goals, NASA brought in the best people for each job. The first ball in space may have been Soviet, but Americans were soon playing golf on the moon.

YOUR ROUTE TO THE TOP...
WAYS TO BUILD NEW TEAM TRUST

Create connections. Give natural synergy a nudge by matching the tempo of your new colleague's voice, nodding when they nod or imitating their stance. But don't overdo it.

Be bland. Don't compete with egos or eccentrics, especially early on. Irreverent statements and passionate outbursts may impress some, but an even temper, considered contributions and an inclusive approach win the trust of many.

Define your direction. The employees of a fledgling Fujifilm were quickly united by a simple aim: 'Kill Kodak'. Develop a mission statement together early, then set benchmark goals to make it happen. Shared accountability accelerates trust.

Ditch the niceties. Forging a bond with awaydays and Friday drinks? Don't bother. Delivering on professional promises builds trust quicker. Quit small talk and start hitting deadlines.

Banish ambiguity. Misunderstandings breed mistrust. Reach an agreed way of working. Clarify 'hygiene factors' (hours, sickness), communication (face-to-face meetings, e-mail) and other customs (problem-solving, conflict management).

Open up. Struggling with your budget? Ashamed of your Excel ineptitude? Admitting weaknesses to your team deepens intimacy and helps you develop complementary skill sets.

Let go. Former GE chair Jack Welch said: 'If you pick the right people and give them the opportunity to spread their wings, you almost don't have to manage them.' Nervous new team leaders: relinquish control and watch staff prove their worth.

Share the weight. Whether it's a missed target, an angry client or a failed negotiation, treat individuals' mistakes as team issues and deal with the fallout together.

Be patient. Developing trust takes time.

Jack Welch was right – tempting though it might be to try to keep everything under control yourself – you will ultimately fail (and find yourself in bad health) if you don't let go of the reins.

ARE YOU SUFFERING FROM... MADONNA SYNDROME?

Do you have a tendency to be bossy? Are everyone's standards beneath yours? Do people who eat or drink too much repel you? In fact, do you hate anyone who doesn't share your views (on anything, even though yours keep changing)? It was going to happen; sooner or later they were going to medicalise Madonna fairly or not, to give a catchy new label to an old phenomenon. She of the two-hour daily workout and macrobiotic diet would never understand those whose gym membership lapsed ten years ago. Another word for control freak, Madonna Syndrome describes people who have a tendency to order for everyone in a restaurant (though no one asked them to). They make lists, leave Post-it notes all over the house and never forget a detail. There is no such thing as a loose arrangement or a spontaneous moment with a Madonna Syndrome sufferer. Treatment requires a letting go of the reins, as they say. Psychotherapy and drugs can help with symptoms (which are based on the fear of being out of control), but not as much as a long holiday and a few stiff drinks. Then, who cares what happens.

TO BOLDLY GO...

'Nothing is more difficult to initiate than a new order of things'
NICCOLÒ MACHIAVELLI SAID IT

As a leader, people will expect you to behave in a certain way. What that way is will depend on the organisation you work for, the sector you work in and it might even be based on how your predecessor behaved. But it's important to remember that although your behaviour should be appropriate to your circumstances, there's no reason why you can't do things your way – if it gets results. Don't be scared to be different.

But a quick aside for those of you who have never been in a leadership position before, especially if you are worried about being taken seriously by the people who yesterday were your mates, and who today you lead. Remind yourself that you have authority over them now, and even if you are the most laid-back boss in the world, they need to take *you* seriously.

YOUR ROUTE TO THE TOP...
ACQUIRING GRAVITAS

Think about your natural body space, then imagine it is twice as great, then imagine it fills the whole room. Hold that thought and your body language will automatically increase your presence.

Talk at a measured pace – gushing suggests gullible; steady suggests wise. Don't raise your voice. Stop talking when you've made your point, even if there is silence. Don't worry if it takes others time to understand you.

Look slightly above the people you are talking to, as if the point you are making is more important than their reaction.

Change the role you are playing if you're having trouble gaining gravitas. If the other people know more than you, provide incisive summaries or ask challenging questions rather than compete in an area where you can't shine.

Set the mood – be the source of enthusiasm if the others are sombre, or the voice of calm consideration if the rest are ebullient.

Don't talk over other people or, if you have to, wait until there is silence before you make any serious points.

Give your undivided attention when others are speaking – at least, to start with.

Focus on quality rather than quantity. People with presence say relatively little, but what they say counts.

Take a few notes. It suggests you are sifting the gems or having brilliant thoughts (high presence). But furious scribbling will make others see you as the note-taker.

Don't expect to be liked – gravitas is for gaining respect; if it's love you want, try building rapport, which requires the opposite of many of these techniques.

EARLY DAYS

The inevitable settling-in period can be daunting. Your every move will be scrutinised, your every foible uncovered, your every word analysed. Even the type of coffee you like will have a bearing on others' perceptions of you. Do you want to be a skinny mochaccino or a blast-your-head-off double-shot espresso?

Your early days as a leader are likely to be exhilarating and nerve-racking but it's critical that you get it right because first impressions can last a lifetime. If ever you should follow the courage of your convictions, it's now.

It's time to be brave and act bold…

WORDS-WORTH:
RISK

'Risk' is a situation involving exposure to danger or, at least, the chance that something unpleasant will happen. The word in English dates back to the seventeenth century, when it was spelled 'risque', indicating its French origin. That seems to have come from the Italian risco, *itself derived from a verb* riscare, *'to run into danger'. Early uses referred to the real dangers of life (being hanged, for instance), but it took on a commercial meaning in the eighteenth century, when it described the chance of losses in insurance and then in business generally. Risk is not just chance but a measurable hazard that can be calculated by using probabilities and the value of any possible losses. In* The Wealth of Nations *(1776), Adam Smith made the classic statement of the meaning of risk in business: 'The ordinary rate of profit always rises more or less with the risk.' Entrepreneurs take risks and are rewarded for it. So do (and are) bankers, but they often employ an excellent method for dealing with risk: they use other people's money.*

If you're going to make an impact, then you are going to have to be brave. It might mean saying 'no' more times than you like or taking a courageous decision without everyone's backing. But that's the job of the leader – to stick your neck out and do what is best for your organisation, even if that does put a few noses out of joint.

'The art of leadership is saying no, not yes'
TONY BLAIR SAID IT

History lessons: Rupert Murdoch

As Goethe said: 'Boldness has genius, power and magic.' It has taken some unbelievably audacious decisions to put Rupert Murdoch imperiously on the world's media throne. The Battle of Wapping in 1986, when he beat the all-powerful print unions, defined his courage. But his tenacity had always been there. Whether he's a young whelp transforming the Australian newspapers he's just inherited, a seasoned proprietor making the *Sun* the loudest voice in the British press, or taking a risk by charging readers for *The Times* and the *Sunday Times* online, he never ducks a difficult decision. The News Corporation empire is now taken for granted, but each step into a new field took ruthless nerve and in lesser hands might have failed – from BSkyB to Fox News. A former Murdoch broadsheet editor sums up: 'He doesn't just see over the hill. He sees over the whole Himalayas.'

Foresight is one thing, but you need the courage to capitalise on it...

YOUR ROUTE TO THE TOP...
BECOME A BRAVE LEADER

Feel the fear. Courageous leaders experience as much fear as others; they just don't let it paralyse them. Replace 'I can't' with 'I will'.

Say it like it is. Authentic communication can be a challenge, especially when the message is tough, or you don't believe in it. But what people want is the truth. This doesn't mean being perfect, it just means doing your best to be real, warts and all.

Have hope. Randy Pausch, a professor at Carnegie Mellon University, was diagnosed with pancreatic cancer. His last lecture could have been a depressing experience; instead it was life-affirming. Look to the future, no matter how turbulent the current circumstances. As Pausch himself said: 'Brick walls are there to remind you how much you want something.'

Talk to yourself. Challenge your catastrophic fantasies. Give answers to your 'what ifs'. Scrutinise any unhelpful thoughts.

Don't give up. Turnaround champions and entrepreneurs alike agree on one thing: persistence lies at the heart of success.

Stand tall. In a world of consensus-building and endless collaboration, brave leaders inspire their followers with decisive action. To be brave is to be in control. Put an end to dithering and offer clear direction to your team.

Live a vital life. Great athletes tend to project enormous vitality. So do great leaders. Create an infectious mood that will win over the cynics – as well as invigorate the evangelists.

Be humble with success. In his book *Good to Great*, Jim Collins demonstrates a negative correlation between the fame of a CEO and their business performance. Ask for honest feedback, let others shine and selectively share weaknesses. Top leaders build enduring greatness through professional will and personal humility.

History lessons: Horatio Nelson

Admiral Lord Nelson led from the front and bore the scars to prove it (losing an arm and an eye – that's more than mere flesh wounds). His fiery spirit and delight in battle captured the nation's imagination and made him a legend in his own time. Consider his bold approach in the Battle of Copenhagen in 1801. Three years after his spectacular victory at the Nile, this was another toughie: the Danish fire was so punishing that Nelson's superior ordered him to retreat. But Nelson didn't like to turn his back on a challenge. He famously raised his telescope to his blind eye and announced: 'I really do not see the signal!' – more popularly misquoted as 'I see no ships' – and carried on fighting. He won, of course. This approach is highly risky: he would have had a royal ticking-off had his reckless attitude sent his men to slaughter. But Nelson, like any good leader, knew that fortune favours the brave. When the glory's there for the taking, it's often wise to turn a blind eye to sobering facts and battle on.

Brave leaders take brave decisions – or at least they know how to make a decision quickly and well. For those of you who need reminding:

CRASH COURSE IN...
MAKING GOOD DECISIONS

Frame it. The first step is to define the decision. Most decisions go wrong because the wrong issue requiring a decision is identified – the symptoms rather than the true causes are addressed. Decisions can be stimulated by three situations: opportunity, problem resolution and crisis. They need to be framed in terms of a well-defined problem, which usually means travelling from the current clearly described situation to the desired situation.

Whose decision? Ask yourself: is it important to make a decision? And if I don't make the decision, will it be made by someone else? If your answer is 'yes' to the first and 'no' to the second, you either have to take the decision or delegate it.

Understand your mind. How do you make decisions? Most decision-making depends on two main processes. The first is pattern-recognition, when your decision-making is influenced by how you dealt with a similar situation from the past. It is based on your previous experience. The second process is emotional tagging, which involves an emotional investment being attached to particular outcomes. So you'll favour one outcome over another because you perceive that it will make you happier.

Question your objectivity. In each case, you may have in-built biases you aren't aware of. You favour a particular course of action because that's how it was done in your previous job, or perhaps you have a personal interest in the decision: e.g., relocating an office nearer your own home. If there is a risk of bias creeping in, you need to introduce safeguards that will counterbalance it.

Sharpen your skills. Consider the widest range of options. People find it easier to look at one plan at a time, but you can progress and evaluate several simultaneously. 'Research has demonstrated the value of counter-factual thinking,' says Gary Marcus, professor of psychology at New York University, in his book *Kluge*. 'Thinking about the opposite helps us make better decisions.'

Share the burden. Form a decision-making group, and subject its activity to oversight – say, by the board. McKinsey has found that firms good at decision-making share the process and allow dissent along the way.

Don't write off intuition. We make certain types of decision better intuitively than analytically. Nimble firms leave day-to-day decision-making with instinctive leaders who can make rapid calls on most issues, but subject difficult and bias-ridden decisions to a procedural method.

Do say: 'We have a comprehensive approach to cover all our strategic decision-making requirements.'

Don't say: 'Ip, dip, penny, chip ...'

So, you've worked up some courage; now it's time to get on with the job. First impressions count for a lot and it's imperative that you storm your first 100 days.

Masterclass in the First-100-days Plan:
What are they?
New hires and the newly promoted often find themselves being judged after the apparently arbitrary deadline of 100 days. The figure has a plausible roundness to it, hinting at something significant. You might feel that business life has got fast enough already, without having to deliver meaningful change in just over three months. On the other hand, the markets expect quarterly figures from most companies, so maybe 100 days is not such a weird deadline. Blame Jack Kennedy if you want. At his inauguration in 1961, he spoke explicitly of the nation's expectations for his first 100 days – there was no looking back after that.

Where did they come from?
In fact, it was an earlier US president who got the 100-day bandwagon rolling. When Franklin D. Roosevelt entered the White House in the wake of the Depression of the early 1930s, he instigated a radical 100-day plan to reform the failing US economy. Talk about a 'burning platform' for change! Crucially, he inspired a sceptical nation with his leadership and bold rhetoric – 'I tell you we have nothing to fear except fear itself', and so on. Ever since, new leaders have found their efforts judged at the 100-day landmark. Artificial, perhaps, but irresistible. New leaders will never be able to escape this 100-day litmus test.

You may have a faultless, high-impact first-100-days plan but you're not going to achieve anything unless you've got the right people on side. It's time to brush up on your political intelligence…

Masterclass in Political Quotient: What is it?

Yes, just what we needed: a new acronym for business. We've had IQ, EQ, even SQ – social intelligence – and now here comes PQ: political quotient, or intelligence. The idea behind this label is that complex, political organisations – and have you ever known one that wasn't political? – have to be navigated with care, subtlety and intelligence. Knowing where the power lies and how to grab some of it are key survival skills. This is about more than mere tact and courtesy; this is about plotting a path to the top and avoiding getting shafted.

Where did it come from?

The business writer Jo Owen coined the term in his book *Power at Work*. He has a clear-sighted view of relationships in the workplace. But, cleverly, he does not see the search for power as a solo performance or an ego trip. 'The reality is that power does not lie with the individual: it lies in the power of the system,' Owen writes. That comment is the mark of a person with high PQ. Use the power networks that already exist; don't try to fight them or supersede them. That way madness lies. Politics is not going to go away any time soon. And it could be that as organisations become more global, we'll all need to hone our political skills and understanding even more. Those who succeed in this diverse, cross-border future will have what the psychologist Howard Gardner calls a 'synthesising mind' – people who are able to deal with various influences and ideas, grasp lots of different 'vibes' and cultures, and master them. You will have to mind your Ps, your Qs, and your PQ.

There might be aspects of your job that involve challenges of a personal kind. One of the most common is public speaking. You might find yourself called upon to represent your team, department or organisation at an industry event. Or you might be hauled up in front of investors, shareholders, customers or any other stakeholder. It's time to bite the bullet…

THE LEADERSHIP MASTERCLASS

CRASH COURSE IN...
PUBLIC SPEAKING

Seek help. This is one area where coaching really helps. Finding your best voice is largely a matter of mechanics, but you need somebody to watch, listen and tell you where you are going wrong.

Plan it. Sounds obvious, but start by deciding your key message. This enables you to make a structure (e.g., tell them what you're going to tell them; tell them; tell them what you told them), which is a first step to dispelling your nerves. A clear structure is the skeleton that keeps everything together.

Relax. Start with breathing. It provides the power behind your voice, and enables you to achieve what is called 'active relaxation' – so that you are not nervous but are in control. Most people need to slow down their delivery. Take time and enjoy the words.

Give your voice a workout. The aim is to get your voice firing on all cylinders, so you achieve good enunciation, projection, variety of expression and so on. You want to engage the audience, not sound boring. It's a purely physical thing, like going to a vocal gym.

Put it in points. It's time to write what you're going to say. But avoid having your speech scripted down to the last word – the audience will switch off. Bullet points, mnemonics and cards are useful devices. Learn the first three sentences off by heart. It means you won't start off by um-ing and er-ing.

Cut out the funny stuff. Unless you're a natural comedian and you know the audience well, it's best to steer clear of jokes. If your joke falls flat, it's much harder to pick yourself up, and you can easily offend someone. Better to include lots of examples – they add colour and engage the audience's imagination.

Practise, practise, practise. You can't rehearse too many times. And on the day? Arrive early and familiarise yourself with the space. Don't drink alcohol beforehand, but make sure you have some water to hand. When you step up on stage, don't think about how you're feeling, think about the job you have to do. And if you panic, remember the golden rule: 'When in doubt, breathe out.'

Do say: 'First, let me tell you what I'm going to talk about today.'

Don't say: 'Before I start, has anyone heard the one about the Muslim, the Christian and the Jew who went to a lap-dancing club…'

So, you've covered the basics – now a word of warning about a couple of syndromes for the novice leader to watch out for:

ARE YOU SUFFERING FROM… INFORMATION COMPULSION?

No sooner have you finished the newspaper than you go on to Bloomberg to make sure you haven't missed an update. All such things are, of course, programmed into your BlackBerry to make sure you don't miss a single turn in the stock market or a new riot in Bangkok. In fact, you have one of those watches with three time-settings just because you need to know who is awake to e-mail the latest news if the BlackBerry bleeps in the middle of the night. Compulsion is... well, uncontrollable behaviour you keep repeating, and information is something we all have too much of. Add them up and you get the picture. People in the throes of this disorder feel out of touch in a matter of seconds. Missing the news – even of an opening of a restaurant (in Siberia) – creates a sense of loss. Like an addict, the sufferer needs more and more to feel better, but even that is never enough. Cold turkey is too dramatic a cure: weaning the addict slowly, first off the wires and then off the second edition of the same paper, is a start.

Or...

ARE YOU SUFFERING FROM... CONTINUOUS PARTIAL ATTENTION?

Secretly checking your iPhone in mid-conversation? Writing a document but really looking out for incoming e-mails? You turned off the sound, but you can still see who's there, of course. Continuous Partial Attention is the plague of our time. It's the ability to be there but not in full, to listen with one ear elsewhere and to concentrate without actually concentrating – the office equivalent of the cocktail party look-over-your-shoulder technique. Coined by a Microsoft executive (funny, that), it is the opposite of multi-tasking – more like semi-tasking, where responding to a text seems more critical than listening to your children discuss their day at school. The source of all the trouble is of course technology – it's just too tempting to check who an e-mail is from. The cure, apart from throwing out the laptop and sticking the iPhone in the fridge, is to limit the hits to specific times and adopt what they call a counter-addiction – say, smoking.

ONCE YOU'VE HIT YOUR STRIDE...

The first few months are done and dusted – you've proved yourself to be a capable leader and there have been no major cock-ups on your watch. 'Yes,' you might think to yourself, 'I'm pretty good at what I do. Come to think of it, my organisation is mighty lucky to have me at all. I'm going to sit back on my laurels and watch my minions dance to my tune.' Stop and ask yourself: 'Is it time to rein in that huge ego of mine?'

YOUR ROUTE TO THE TOP...
CONTROL YOUR EGO

Concentrate on the outcome. Remember, it's the result that matters rather than your role in it. Searching for glory will only damage your chance of success.

Let others speak. Listen to their views and allow them to influence yours. A moment of silence once they've finished is worth a hundred interruptions while they're still talking.

Be generous. As the saying goes: 'If you catch too many fish, the best place to store them is in another person's stomach.' If colleagues feel they've gained from your achievements they will love you all the more.

Try modesty. You may be feeling good about what you have achieved but you don't have to tell everyone how great you are.

Treat people equally. Whether you are the boss, the client or the expert in the field, recognise that others have as much to contribute, just in different ways.

Be impartial. When someone asks for personal advice, put your own agenda to one side and base your recommendations on what you think is really in their best interest.

Spread your thanks liberally. Make a noise about the contributions your colleagues have made. Name them, and be specific about what they did so well. The appreciation will come back to you – perhaps when you really need it.

Adapt to criticism. It doesn't have to be wholeheartedly accepted, but enough to show that you are willing to change.

Fall down. All successful leaders show they are fallible. Allow yourself to make mistakes; these are the vitamins of learning and a powerful indicator of lasting leadership.

Draw your confidence from elsewhere. Don't let your identity be based entirely on how well you're doing at work. Self-esteem gains its strength from all parts of life.

Now's the time to hone the finer details of your leadership style and to learn or brush up the skills that'll keep you at the top. One of the most important is your ability to motivate your top team to give their best…

Ten Ways to be a Motivator

1 Set clear, achievable goals
2 Listen
3 Give praise
4 Use incentives...
5 ... and deliver on them
6 Give pep talks
7 Celebrate triumphs...
8 ... but don't dwell on failures
9 Stand up for the team
10 Buy the first round

'If you are going through hell, keep going'
WINSTON CHURCHILL SAID IT

If you've enjoyed a smooth run in your new leadership role – congratulations! Take time to enjoy it because it's not going to last for ever. Sooner or later you're going to face a situation that will test your skills to an uncomfortable level. What to do?

ARE YOU SUFFERING FROM... INTERMITTENT EXPLOSIVE DISORDER?

Every office has one: the door-slamming hot-head whose secretary is always in tears. One minute he's all smiles, and the next he's pointing his BlackBerry directly at someone's head. Intermittent Explosive Disorder is often diagnosed when the aggression is much more dramatic than the incident that

provoked it. Sufferers don't moderate their annoyance but go from nought to 100 in less time than it took to say: 'Sorry, couldn't finish the project.' There's often assault and a destructive component, evidenced by the state of the office furniture. Few wish to work for someone with Intermittent Explosive Disorder, yet sufferers are surprisingly apt at getting up the greasy pole, because everyone fears their temper. No one wants to be the idiot who said: 'Now, now, settle down.' Treatment is best left to the men in white coats who carry pills with them. The problem is: as soon as they arrive, the sufferer is all smiles again.

YOUR ROUTE TO THE TOP...
KEEP YOUR COOL

Consider the cost benefits. Those skilled at self-control aren't just more popular than their fiery colleagues, they're more successful too. In a study of partners at a management consultancy, the biggest difference in profitability lay in their levels of self-control. Lash out or cash in? The choice is yours.

Identify the source. If your control-freak MD leaves you fuming, launch a pre-emptive strike. Schedule a meeting at the start of each project to agree when, where and how he or she will provide input. They'll be a lot less infuriating when you're working on your terms.

Imagine the consequences. Your colleague smugly highlights an error in the hefty report you've just completed. Before you let them have it ('Who asked you? Can't you keep your opinions to yourself for once?'), fast-forward a week. The prospect of frosty silences and no partner for the high-profile pitch should be enough to hold you back.

Talk to the page. Expressing our emotions on paper makes us more self-aware and less likely to lash out. Keep a diary of your thoughts and feelings every day for a month and achieve Gandhi-like calm.

Stop digging. Fiery people can be pacified by finding a pattern to their anger. Something has to trigger it – a particular concern, person or time of day. Identify situations that make you angry and avoid them.

Look for the best. When the red mist descends, try to find a positive explanation for the other person's behaviour. 'My colleague is shouting at me not because he is a bully, but because he's panicked about the bleak projected figures.'

Run, punch a cushion, rant. Do whatever it takes to calm the beast. Just don't do it at work.

Much more effective than exploding at anyone who disagrees with you is to get your way in a smarter manner.

YOUR ROUTE TO THE TOP...
HOW TO GET YOUR WAY

Keep your enemies close. Let the other person speak first. You'll gain invaluable insights into their true concerns and they'll be more likely to listen when it's your turn.

Delve deep. Ask questions to find out what's driving them. Whether they want to be inspired or to be given irrefutable facts, you can adapt your approach once you know their motivations.

Engage them. Be clear about what's in it for them: 'This project will involve working closely with a number of different people. I believe this will appeal to your social side.' People make decisions for their own reasons, not yours.

Choose your words carefully. Use phrases like: 'let's...' or 'shall we try...?' If you're pushy, they'll be less likely to comply.

Flattery will get you everywhere. To get a colleague to adopt the next proposal, explain what was good about the last one and why: 'The industry examples work really well and I like the humorous tone.' If they feel favourably towards you, they'll be more open to persuasion. Just don't overdo it.

Guide them. People are most likely to agree to something if they feel they've come to the conclusion themselves. In *My Big Fat Greek Wedding*, the protagonist's mother uses gentle questioning to get her way. It's so effective that the daughter leaves to follow her dreams, and her father thinks it was his idea.

Make your case. State all the facts, and be clear about the pros and cons. Offer solutions that will resolve their concerns and open a debate to incorporate their views. Focus on areas where it's easier to adapt without damaging the integrity of what you're trying to achieve.

Be prepared to compromise. Is your way really the best way? Present your proposal as a first draft to work on together. A collaborative solution is more likely to lead to a positive outcome for everyone.

Knowing how to get your own way is a useful skill to have when dealing with outside stakeholders.

WORDS-WORTH: STAKEHOLDER

Gone are the days when a leader could safely assume that a 'stakeholder' was a minor character in a Dracula movie. These days it means someone who may not own a company but has an interest in its fortunes and so has to be taken into consideration: employees, customers and neighbours. A 'stake' has long had two meanings. From Anglo-Saxon times it was a length of wood used, say, in burning heretics or dealing firmly with the undead. Since the 1500s it has also meant a sum of money put up to be taken by the winner of a race or a gamble. A 'stakeholder', first recorded in 1815, was a trusted third party who held the stake until the contest was decided. 'Stakeholder' in our sense (often used in contrast to 'stockholder' or 'shareholder') was coined in the 1960s but is associated with R. Edward Freeman, author of Strategic Management: A stakeholder approach *(1984). Freeman is an expert in business ethics, as most managers will have to become. 'Stakeholder' is an idea that is not going to lie down in its coffin.*

History lessons: Marie Antoinette

Born Maria Antonia Josefa Johanna von Habsburg-Lothringen in 1755, fifteenth child of the emperor and empress of the Holy Roman Empire, Marie Antoinette left Vienna at fifteen to marry the French Dauphin. Out of her depth in the murky French court, and urged by her family to push Austria's interests, her marriage remained unconsummated for seven years. She consoled herself with retail therapy, splashing out on diamonds, backing horses and having her own village built. She may never have uttered the line 'Let them eat cake', but she certainly had her slice and ate it – as her French subjects starved. Such extravagance was not new to European royalty, but its timing was bad, and 'Madame Deficit' soon followed her husband to the scaffold.

Business royalty has made the same mistake – just look at Conrad Black. Neglect your stakeholders at your peril. Let the office fall to ruin while wining and dining your non-execs and see what happens. It could be 'off with your head'...

Bearing this in mind...

DO IT RIGHT:
YOUR NEXT AGM

Plan. Talk to your board beforehand and allocate areas of expertise for the Q&A session. Don't let your resident limelight-stealer poach questions.

Work the floor. Get your corporate communications team out there. Have them talk to the shareholders – and not just 'hello' and 'goodbye'. You won't get a better opportunity to find out what they're thinking.

Include the newbies. Send a special reminder out to anyone who has become a shareholder in the past year. And make a point of talking to them.

Rethink the agenda. It doesn't have to be the same every year. Give your audience reasons to stay awake. It needn't be the CEO who gives the keynote presentation. Had a year of mergers? Get the M&A director on stage.

Use your board. You don't pay your non-execs all that money just to rock up to five or six meetings a year. Send them out to meet the shareholders – and not just the key ones – during the AGM.

Get the branding right. Too much, and they'll worry that you're wasting their money. Too little, and, again, they'll worry that you're wasting their money. It's all about keeping them confident in the brand.

Enjoy it. Don't leave your shareholders feeling that you held the AGM under duress. Make them feel that you wanted to share the company's success with them. She might look like some sweet old lady, but you couldn't have done it without her money.

STRATEGY

'Change is not a destination, just as hope is not
a strategy'
RUDY GIULIANI SAID IT

A strategy is defined as 'a particular long-term plan for success'
– and every leader needs to have one. This can be daunting
for the novice, who might be more practised in executing
a strategy than in devising one, so it's time to get up to
speed on some of the basics so that you can keep your head
above water.

THE NEED TO KNOW ESSENTIALS

'There is nothing wrong with change, if it is in the
right direction'
WINSTON CHURCHILL SAID IT

Change – good and bad – is a constant in life and business
and every strategy must be premised on it. As a leader, you
must not only be comfortable with change, it should be
something that you can handle confidently – and even enjoy.

YOUR ROUTE TO THE TOP...
MANAGING CHANGE

Start with yourself. It isn't the changes that do you in, it's the transitions. In other words, problems lie not in the new role or structure but in how you adjust. The better you manage your own transition, the easier it is to guide others.

Get stuck in. Planning is helpful but not when it becomes a reason to procrastinate. You're unlikely to create a perfect plan, and even if you did, it wouldn't stay perfect for long.

Find the means. Archimedes said: 'Give me a lever and I will move the world.' Whether it's changing a process, merging two teams or empowering staff to make decisions, what levers can you use to support that change?

Create ownership. In 2008, two million Americans became infected with a serious illness in hospital; of those, 90,000 died. It was all because medical staff weren't washing their hands enough. The hospital tried charts, spreadsheets and disinfectant wipes to no effect, then started listening to staff. The result: better engagement and lasting behavioural change.

Embody the change. When Fabio Capello inherited England's football team in 2008, its over-indulged and privileged stars were said to run the show. No-nonsense Capello reignited competition for places and restored the key focus: what happens on the pitch. And no one questions who's in charge.

Relish resistance. Letting sceptics air their views and addressing their concerns will bring them on board. You might even learn a thing or two.

Tell it like it is. Research shows that in times of turbulence, people want above all else to see authenticity in their leaders.

Recognise and reward. Whether it's a public expression of thanks, a team lunch or an early Friday finish, acknowledge milestones along the way to add momentum and advertise success.

Some change will be more extreme than others. Take the radical condition that is known as the corporate turnaround. This is when the fortunes of a business are so dire that the only way out of an early grave is by enforcing massive change to kick-start a recovery. Be prepared for some extensive surgery.

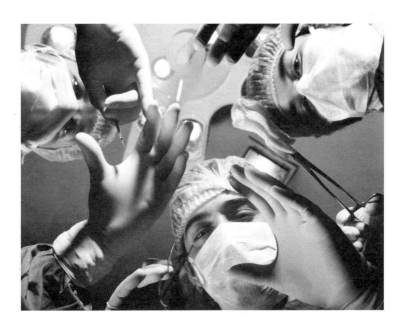

Masterclass in Corporate Turnaround: What is it?

'Buy when there is blood in the streets,' advised Baron Philippe de Rothschild. He was alluding to the fact that economies and markets recover, even from the worst recessions. Firms can be turned round too. That is the good news. The tougher part is taking the necessary measures that will make recovery possible. These have to do with cutting costs and getting real about future revenue streams, but also taking calculated risks on levels of future demand. This is a good time to start getting those turnaround strategies in place.

Where did it come from?

Few companies last for ever. Those that have survived for several decades have almost all come back from near-death experiences. Rolls-Royce, Britain's great engineering champion, was saved by Edward Heath's government in the early 1970s. Many British banks have had to be bailed out before, or have lost fortunes in the developing world. The most famous turnaround of recent years took place at computer giant IBM. Taking over in 1993, CEO Lou Gerstner has said of his time there that 'Transformation of an enterprise begins with a sense of crisis or urgency.' Turnaround experts are very busy. The credit crunch has deprived many weaker businesses of regular funding streams. The financial tide has gone out and, as Warren Buffett says, now we will get to see who has been swimming naked. It's bye-bye to fat expenses, failing subsidiaries, obsolete products and underperforming colleagues. Just one question: why did we wait until now to deal with such things?

'What's dangerous is not to evolve'
JEFF BEZOS SAID IT

A leader must never let their team or organisation rest on its laurels. As soon as complacency takes hold, it'll spread like the Bubonic Plague. You must create a strategy that has innovation at its heart because sticking with the status quo guarantees only one thing: regression, not progression. The only way to stay top dog is to innovate…

Masterclass in Innovation:
What is it?
There's nothing new about innovation. Adam's fig-leaf, the wheel and man-made fire were all historically significant examples of it. In business, innovation has long been regarded as a silver bullet, an essential step to beating the competition and winning market share. But often businesses have been managed almost as if to stamp out the potential for new ideas. No wonder Tom Peters and Bob Waterman, in their classic book *In Search of Excellence*, described the action required before innovation can take place as: 'Ready, Fire, Aim'.

Where did it come from?
It is human nature to innovate. Experimentation, trying and failing, is how progress has always been made. We have an irresistible urge to discover the next new thing for fear of being left behind. Business leaders are not the only people to exploit this. Tony Blair didn't storm to power at the head of something called Same Old Labour. In his books *The Innovator's Dilemma* and *The Innovator's Solution*, Clayton Christensen identifies 'disruptive' or 'sustaining' innovations that shake up or develop the market for specific goods and services. All through the value chain are areas where more

money could be made with innovative solutions. The message is: look for products and markets where complacent incumbents are failing to innovate successfully. And disrupt them before someone comes along to disrupt you.

And innovation requires initiative…

WORDS-WORTH:
INITIATIVE

Initiative, the initiative, an initiative: all different, all important in business. 'Initiative' is the ability to act independently; 'the initiative' is what you take when you take the first step; and 'an initiative' is a bureaucrat's scheme for addressing a problem. The first is what we'd most like, but the third is what we usually get. Government has initiatives the way dogs have fleas – on teeth-brushing, home insulation, breakfast, smoking, number plates, getting women back to work, bright children, alcohol, starter homes, higher education, chewing gum, ending world poverty … 'Initiative' began as the Latin initium, meaning 'entrance' or 'beginning'; it has been used in English since the late eighteenth century. But the modern term is an American variant. Many US state constitutions incorporate 'initiatives', letting citizens start off legislation, and this led to the use of the word for important government actions. They get the Strategic Defense Initiative (aka Star Wars) and we get… the Home Composting Initiative.

YOUR ROUTE TO THE TOP...
MAKE YOUR IDEAS FLY

Get ranking. Decide what criteria a new idea must meet (will increase sales), should meet (will save us time), and might meet (will boost engagement). Score your ideas according to how many 'must', 'should' and 'might' boxes they tick and cull the bottom 50 per cent. Ruthlessness now will save vital time and cost later.

Choose life. Consider what will help each idea live (the chairman of the board came up with it, it aligns with organisational values) and what could kill it (the financial director has frozen expenditure on this issue, something similar has failed before). Ditch doomed ideas, no matter how brilliant they seem.

Trust your intuition. It is based on years of experience about what works for you.

Step into new shoes. How would a lawyer, inventor or artist rate your suggestions? What would excite or concern them? Interrogate your ideas from their perspectives to unearth a fresh set of pluses and pitfalls.

Remember your rejects. Struggling to shortlist your ideas? Revisit those that were culled earlier and ask yourself why. Reconfirming what won't work helps to clarify what will.

Take the right risks. Eli Broad, founder of the financial services retirement specialist SunAmerica, made his billions by 'embracing risk, as long as it was well thought out and, in a worst-case scenario, I'd still land on my feet'. Consider the risk:reward ratio of your ideas and progress only those whose failure wouldn't finish you.

Choose allies wisely. Initiatives flourish or flounder according to who is brought into the concept. Share your ideas with the organisation's powerful players, highlighting the elements they'll find most engaging.

Act now. From accountability for tasks to timeframes for completion, map out exactly what needs to happen to bring your idea to life. Rigorous evaluation is worthless without robust implementation.

Keep your eyes peeled. Don't switch off once your idea is rolling out. According to economist Israel Kirzner, the defining skill of successful tycoons is 'entrepreneurial alertness': the ability to constantly scan the market horizon for opportunities and innovations. What's your next pearl?

Any red-blooded capitalist will tell you that the key to success is growth. A leader will be judged on this. How will you grow the opportunity for your organisation? How will you expand your business?

Masterclass in Expansion:
What is it?

The idea that businesses should try to get bigger is a fundamental tenet of capitalism. To be labelled 'ex-growth' by City analysts is a cue for a calamitous fall in your share price. Businesses should try to grow, the theory runs, because competitors will always try to steal your market share. A firm that is not expanding is therefore, by definition, contracting. Expansion is an even bigger priority for start-ups and entrepreneurs; in fact, it's everything.

Where did it come from?

It's a concept of the industrial age. When businesses were essentially local and small-scale – think agriculture, skilled craftspeople and traders – there was no need to grow beyond your known territory. Indeed, this is the sustainable model that many Greens would like us to return to. But with the coming of mechanised big business and the spread of the railways – all in the context of growing national empires – the whole world became a marketplace. It was capitalism's manifest destiny to grow into it. Since then the race has been on to grow and grow. But what the world needs now is 'green growth'. A contradiction in terms? Maybe not. Not many people are going to vote for zero or negative economic growth, and yet nearly everyone now accepts that the expansion of our own and the global economy has to take place in a sustainable manner. The management writer Charles Handy has asked another pertinent question: who says you have to get bigger? Do the vineyards of Château Pétrus have to get bigger? Should the London Symphony Orchestra have 20 per cent more violins next year? Perhaps 'better, not bigger' is a more helpful organisational goal.

One way of achieving 'better' and 'bigger' is by attracting more investment into your organisation. But how to do it? Expansion can also mean acquisition. Mergers and acquisitions (M&A) are back, and there are bargains to be had – if you can get your hands on the cash.

Ten Ways to Attract an Investor

1 Understand your company
2 Know your goals and how to achieve them
3 Consider the options
4 Be ready to hand over the reins
5 Recognise your weaknesses
6 Keep a lid on budgets
7 Get advice
8 Check their record and references
9 Make sure they fit...
10 ... and that they can afford you

Masterclass in Mergers and Aquisitions (M&A): What is it?

It's a jungle out there. Kill or be killed. This is the iron law of business. Get big or die trying: merge, acquire or lose out. Every company has its price, and if you can afford it, a deal can be done. But not before a PR battle gets played out. When one side claims: 'This is a merger of equals, not an acquisition,' don't believe it. Someone will be on top.

Where did it come from?

There have only ever been two ways for a company to grow – 'organically', that is, by winning a greater share of a market through its own efforts, or through mergers or acquisitions. M&A is quicker and seemingly easier than getting better at what you do, but also fraught with difficulty. But deals remain popular – when there's cash to finance them. They are the preferred route for corporate empire-builders. The names of modern firms can betray the extent to which they are the product of deals. For example, GlaxoSmithKline is made up of at least four major drugs companies. And M&A is back. Before stock markets rise any further, acquisitive companies – those with some cash, anyway – will surely look to grab some tasty bargains. The only thing preventing an outbreak of genuine merger mania is the wobbly state of the financial markets. Would you fancy your chances of securing a mega-loan right now?

WHY BUSINESS IS LIKE... MARRIAGE

Mergers are often compared to marriage, which is accurate in one sense, at least – they often fail. Divorce rates are sky-high, and M&A has been said to destroy value in more than 70 per cent of cases, the Daimler/Chrysler and Time Warner/AOL nuptials being prime examples. So it seems curious that M&A is once again on the rise. If our objective is sustainable growth, shouldn't we be looking elsewhere for inspiration? And can the field of human relationships provide any more useful analogies?

Some relationship counsellors suggest cohabitation first – or, in business terms, a strategic alliance, which provides a way to dip a toe in the water. But research indicates that loose arrangements are just as hard to manage and frequently fail. Surprisingly, marriages that follow a period of cohabitation are even more likely to fail, perhaps because of the difficulty of shifting gear from a low-commitment relationship to something deeper. Which is interesting but not very useful if you're looking for a constructive model for growth. So, if neither marriage nor cohabitation offer much other than a warning sign, where should we look next? Maybe polygamy is a better means by which to expand the family unit. Johnson & Johnson, one of the most profitable companies in the world, has never undertaken a major merger, preferring instead to acquire smaller businesses and nurture them rather than absorb them. Its success over 100 years would suggest that this form of getting it on provides a more reliable model for sustainable value creation. We don't recommend that you apply the same rationale to your home life. Unless you live in Salt Lake City.

If M&A is like marriage, then outsourcing is like sending the children off to boarding school. Your business is running smoothly, but overheads are uncompetitive. Is it time to move some functions to a market where labour is cheaper?

CRASH COURSE IN...
OUTSOURCING

Start with strategy. Don't go offshore just because it sounds a good idea. Start with a sourcing strategy that identifies your business drivers and how they can best be delivered.

Weigh the real costs. Cutting payroll cost is an obvious attraction, with 40 to 60 per cent savings typical. But tot up the additional costs of management, training, travel and telecom/IT infrastructure before you decide. Benefit is obtained from economy of scope, not just economy of scale – the higher the proportion of your business moved offshore, the greater the benefit.

In-house or out? Deciding whether to outsource or set up a 'captive' operation overseas is important. Firms are more likely to outsource if they've done it before and if there are suppliers available with the expertise and the cultural match required. If you're an entirely UK-based company, it's a hell of a stretch to think you can go 6,000 miles and set up a new operation from scratch.

Look for a cultural fit. India's low-wage, skill-rich, English-speaking workforce makes it a natural for much going offshore from the UK – but it doesn't fit every bill. If you need people who can build a rapport with your customers over high-price purchases, it may be better to look at, say, South Africa or New Zealand. Shop around.

Take simple steps. The simpler the processes you send offshore, the less there is to go wrong. If you want to re-engineer at the same time, you create an added uncertainty.

Communicate openly. Tell your people what you're planning and why you're doing it. If they understand that you can't recruit the right skills in the UK, or that the competitiveness of the organisation is at stake, they may support it. Follow the consultation rules in the EU Acquired Rights Directive.

Focus on compliance. Data privacy is a big issue when moving operations overseas. Building in the necessary controls is a key part of the transition.

Work out reasonable service levels. Don't sacrifice performance or demand unrealistic improvements when going offshore.

Do say: 'Moving a strategically chosen part of our operation offshore will make us more competitive and ensure a brighter future for our people everywhere.'

Don't say: 'If we airlift everything to Mumbai we'll save a shed-load of cash. We can work out the details later.'

So, there you have some of the basics – enough to keep you going through your first week at least. Once you've settled in, you can get to grips with the additional extras – the nice to knows.

THE NICE TO KNOWS

'As long as you're thinking anyway, think big'
DONALD TRUMP SAID IT

There are a few more strategy terms and concepts that are worth getting to grips with, just to show that you know what you're talking about. The first relates to being more emotionally intelligent – it's gone from being a 'nice to have' quality to a twenty-first-century 'need to have'.

Masterclass in Emotionally Intelligent Strategy: What is it?

You know all those thrilling off-site strategy get-togethers you've had to sit through over the years? The ones with flip charts, SWOT analysis, and earnest, lengthy and circular discussions? They are just so twentieth century. Today, we are into the 'experience economy'. We need to explore the 'deep metaphors' that inspire our customers' spending decisions. This means tuning in better to what might speak to our customers in the marketplace, and devising a strategy that inspires our workforce in the first place. Bingo! – the emotionally intelligent strategy has been born.

Where did it come from?

Much of the credit for this concept goes to the London-based consultancy firm Cognosis. Drawing on its experience of marketing in the drinks and FMCG sectors, Cognosis commissioned research into what managers actually felt about their firm's own strategy-generation. They found that arid, dull strategies were being developed by elite management teams. Middle and junior managers were rarely consulted. There were few reality checks from the shopfloor. The result? Abstract strategies that may have looked sound on paper but won no buy-in from the rest of the organisation. Leadership teams will now have to work a lot harder at developing the emotional appeal of their strategic positioning. They must involve staff at all levels in strategy generation and allow more creative and less hidebound conversations on strategy to develop internally. If it's going to speak to your customers, it will have to speak to your staff first. As Henry Mintzberg has written: 'Strategy doesn't only have to position, it also has to inspire. So an uninspiring strategy is really no strategy at all.'

The best leaders are *au fait* with flexibility. It doesn't mean they can pull off the splits but it does mean they can keep their teams and their organisations nimble and ready to respond to new situations as they arise.

WORDS-WORTH:
ADHOCRACY

'Adhocracy' is a fashionable concept of business organisation. It means a temporary structure devised to deal with a specific problem – a 'task force' is one kind of adhocracy. The word was invented by Alvin Toffler in his 1970 book Future Shock. *Toffler saw it as part of 'a new, free-form world of kinetic organisations' that would 'ultimately supplant bureaucracy', something nobody seems to have told the Civil Service. Ad hoc, a Latin tag meaning 'to this', arrived in Britain in the seventeenth century. Since then, many have adapted it. In the 1930s we had 'ad-hocness', 'ad-hockery' and, later, 'ad-hocism'. Toffler's usage had more lasting impact. In 1990, Robert H. Waterman made it the title of a book. He defined it as 'any organisational form that challenges the bureaucracy in order to embrace the new'. Its latest appearance is in Cory Doctorow's science-fiction novel* Down And Out In The Magic Kingdom, *where Disney World is run as an adhocracy. Yet it would be wrong to call it a Mickey Mouse idea.*

The best organisations not only need to be nimble but they need to be lean. Think toned athlete rather than flabby couch potato.

Masterclass in Lean: What is it?

Relax. Lean is a philosophy, a state of mind and a holistic approach to business, not a low-calorie diet. Lean businesses and organisations are offended by waste – they seek it out and destroy it. They compress production and delivery times, respond quicker to customer demand, and replenish stocks 'just-in-time', without building up unnecessary inventory ('just-in-case') or missing delivery slots ('just-too-late'). Lean is not mean, but it can be green. Lean thinking will cause you to question just about everything you do at work, from morning till night.

Where did it come from?

Lean is a US/Japanese co-production. After the Second World War, General MacArthur drew on quality guru W. Edwards Deming to help rebuild Japanese industry. Deming's approach struck a chord with his hosts, and ironically the insights of the American were to help challenge US economic supremacy in the coming decades. Consultants James Womack and Dan Jones have spread the lean philosophy over the past twenty years. Their books on Toyota's lean production system helped define lean for a new business generation. Womack and Jones have recently published *Lean Solutions*, a development of lean thinking that looks at the customer's preferred way of doing business, and tries to find lean ways of realising it. Tesco is a leading lean player, murdering flabbier competition through a decade-long commitment to lean practices.

You must be the kind of leader who brings their entire organisation together, not keep them hived off from each other in separate silos.

WORDS-WORTH:
SILO

Does your organisation operate 'silos'? Do people have a 'silo mentality'? Can you do anything about 'siloing'? All fascinating questions, and not only in agri-business. A 'silo' in those circles is a chamber for storing grain and other produce. It's a venerable word, dating back to the Ancient Greeks, who kept their corn in a pit known as a siros. *But as a business buzzword, 'silo' has a more distant connection with that bucolic world. To have a 'silo mentality' is to keep things separate, particularly business units or teams. These business 'silos' are vertical units, with their own budgets and hierarchies, and are generally frowned upon. There is a connection with agriculture, but this usage has more sinister origins. Since the late 1950s, a 'silo' has been an underground structure used to house a guided missile, particularly the nuclear kind. These are hardened, costly, destructive and remote enough from each other to make their removal difficult. You can see why 'silos' are not always seen as conducive to good management.*

Hopefully your business has potential but there's no point having a great idea, a great route to market and great sales if your business doesn't have the potential to grow and deliver to meet demand. The best leaders will build this concept into their organisational strategy.

Masterclass in Scalability:
What is it?

OK, you've got a great idea, you know there's a market for it, and the only question is: can you grow fast enough to meet demand? Welcome to the great scalability challenge. As

Peter Sellers' Macmillanesque politician declaimed: 'We must build, but we must build surely.' Financial markets are looking for growth stories. (Being labelled 'ex-growth' is just about the worst insult any analyst can hurl at you.) So the ability to demonstrate not only where the growth is but how you will cope with it is vital.

Where did it come from?

Scalability was one of the hottest buzzwords to emerge in the dot.com boom. The way to pull in lots of lovely venture capital was not just to have a wacky concept for a business; you also had to be able to show how you would have fully staffed outlets all over the world (and on Mars, Saturn and Jupiter) by 2007. 'But is it scalable?' was the acid test. It remains a pretty good question for any start-up. What are the limits to this idea? If it really takes off, will you slip the surly bonds of earth, or just crash and burn? Unless, of course, you are not convinced that unlimited growth is necessarily a good thing. Hospitals and schools want to get better not bigger. Perhaps, in the era of sustainable, green growth, 'better, not bigger' is becoming the new scalability challenge. Can you 'upscale' your quality while keeping the price under control? The evidence seems to suggest that, if the world is to survive, Planet Earth plc may have to go 'ex-growth'.

You must also establish a strategy that makes you stand out from the competition. What makes you different from the rest?

WORDS-WORTH:
DIFFERENTIATION

'Differentiation' means making your product stand out, but that doesn't mean it has to be different. As WPP's CEO Martin Sorrell put it: 'Intangible differentiations are becoming more and more important.' In other words, forget the product, just change the way it's advertised. Note that you 'differentiate' your products so that people can 'differentiate' between them. This ambiguity emerged in the mid-nineteenth century, after the word had been borrowed from mathematics, where it means 'the operation of obtaining a differential or differential coefficient'. It always had scientific meanings. In ecology, it's the process by which a species finds its own niche in a competitive environment. The first relevant citation seems to be in a 1981 New York Times item about Visa. By the 1990s, it had become a business cliché, but that has not halted its progress. Its latest proponents are teachers, who use it to mean giving harder work to brighter children.

Do you want to differentiate yourself by tapping into the premium market?

WORDS-WORTH:
PREMIUM

Adjectives stick to the word 'lager' like feet to a pub carpet. On the street, there's 'cooking', 'throwing' and the notorious 'wife-beater' lager. In the industry, though, they talk about 'premium lager'. In each case, the differentiating factors are price and alcohol content: at the risk of being controversial, that's because price and alcohol content are the only ways of telling lagers apart. As a noun, 'premium' has been around since the seventeenth century. It comes from the Latin praemium, *meaning a payment or reward, and that's one of its meanings today, as well as the sum payable for an insurance policy and, indeed, any earnings or price above the ordinary. As an adjective, it's much more recent, and highly American. It indicates a product of higher quality that commands a higher price. Aside from alcohol, there aren't that many 'premium' products in daily use in Britain: 'premium rate' phone lines, 'premium class' air travel, 'premium unleaded' – and that's about it. As with the lager, the improved quality of these products is in the eye of the beholder; the price hike is real, however.*

Now for the future. The best kind of leader will always have one eye on the present and the other on the horizon...

Masterclass in Forecasting:
What is it?

I knew you were going to ask that. It's only natural – we all want to get ahead of the curve, without going round the bend. For those too impatient to wait for what life has in store for us, there are forecasters, those clever people who seem –

sometimes – to know what is about to happen. But their reputations have taken an almighty hit recently. Hardly anyone seems to have seen the recession coming, or to have been able to imagine how serious it could become. The short-term forecast for forecasters is not good.

Where did it come from?

Pagans studied the entrails of slaughtered beasts to see what the future held. The Celts had their druids, the Romans their soothsayers. But the cynical ancients had got their number. '*Haruspex haruspicem cum videt, ridet*', as they used to say, meaning: 'When one soothsayer sees another, he smiles.' Those modern gurus, newspaper columnists, try their luck, but as Sir Simon Jenkins, a leading exponent of the art, said in the *Guardian*: 'I have no idea what is going to happen over the coming year and nor does anyone else. The futurology game has been shot to ribbons, making fools of everyone.' Who can tell where forecasting is going now? Certainly not the forecasters. But we can't wait to find out what's going to happen. There will always be a role for forecasters, even if they have to rethink their branding ('global strategist', anyone?). But if you ever find yourself wishing that you could just chuck all forecasters into the rubbish bin, along with their stupid predictions, take heart from the wise words of the great management guru, the late Peter Drucker: 'Forecasting is not a respectable human activity, and not worthwhile beyond the shortest periods.'

How can you get ahead of the curve and start spotting trends before they break into the mainstream? The world is changing fast but your firm seems constantly to react after the event. Now's the time to move ahead of the curve.

CRASH COURSE IN...
SPOTTING THE NEXT BIG THING

Understand what trends are... A trend is a change in consumer attitudes or behaviours. The reason you want to predict trends is so your products and services, as well as the channels and attitudes you use in communication, all tie in with these changes. Micro-trends are short-term changes; mega-trends are long-term ones.

... and what they're not. Fads are short-lived products and behaviours that are often driven by marketing; think Cabbage Patch dolls. They might give a clue to an underlying trend, though. If in doubt, is there data to measure the change?

What are you looking for? The first step is to define what drivers are relevant to your business – what sorts of behaviour in the world are crucial to your business doing well. When these have been identified, start experimenting with tracking trends you think might be affecting your business – there are often surprising connections between widely differing areas.

Watch the big picture. Macro trends tend to dictate our environment, often in a broad, sweeping way. Big technological, political, environmental, economic and societal changes will trump consumer trends, which in turn trump industry trends.

Seek far and wide. Don't just look inside your own industry. Many trends start in fashion, design and technology-based industries. Look at media, competitors, research studies, government statistics, online chat and your own customers for the fullest possible data. Tap into a trend-spotting network. Simple, visible, cash-saving trends are more likely to last.

See beyond the headline. We all have access to the same information; the key is to find messages behind the data without losing yourself in meaningless noise. Companies and individuals that add their own perspective and interpretation to a trend make something unique out of it.

Create an innovation culture. Your staff must welcome change. Start a trend group. Convene regular sessions to brainstorm trends and their implications in different parts of the business; focus on one trend and get everyone to come up with ideas for products, business concepts, a change of vision or just the tone of your advertising. Offer rewards for the best ideas.

Do say: 'To survive in a fast-changing world, we must be continually rethinking our strategies and offerings. To do that, we need to identify changes as early as possible.'

Don't say: 'Nah – I can't see a lot happening in the next few years.'

'There's no idea that can't be improved on'
MICHAEL EISNER SAID IT

History lessons: Take the longer view

Ray Kroc stumbled on the McDonald brothers' San Bernardino burger joint in 1954, and soon negotiated a deal to launch a franchise around the US. Unlike most franchisers then and now, Kroc understood the benefit of looking after his franchisees. While the average franchiser was out to get rich quick, slapping large margins on the ingredients they forced licensees to buy, Kroc thought he'd prosper in the long run if he took care of them first. He cut their costs and enforced rigid standards across the board, making their businesses stronger. He charged only $950 for each new restaurant, plus 1.9 per cent of the sales revenue, of which he had to return a quarter to the McDonald brothers. If sales at a branch hit $100k, he'd take home just $1,400. When he bought out the brothers in 1961 for $2.7m, McDonald's had made millionaires of many franchisees. Kroc barely turned a profit, but fast food eventually fed him a $500m fortune. If you want a taste of the bigger stakes, don't chase that quick buck.

REPUTATION

'It takes twenty years to build a reputation and five minutes to ruin it. If you think about that, you'll do things differently'
WARREN BUFFETT SAID IT

Never before has reputation mattered so much in business and society. Trust in big business, banking and institutions is at an all-time low and as a leader, earning a good reputation from your employees, your peers and your customers should be an important consideration.

As an individual, always be vigilant as to how your behaviour and actions will impact on your personal reputation, and the reputation of your organisation. Associate yourself with good things, and the glitter will rub off. Maybe you'll even be lucky enough to suffer from the Halo Effect...

ARE YOU SUFFERING FROM...
THE HALO EFFECT?

The headteacher of a top school stands up in front of a group of parents. They all smile: what an interesting, charming and clever chap he is. The fact that he's stuttering, looking at his feet and saying nothing significant makes no difference. They're hooked. The Halo Effect is the habit many of us have of embellishing another with positive qualities because of his or her association with someone or something successful, whether or not they possess those qualities themselves. It was discovered in 1920 by Edward Thorndike, who interviewed commanding officers about their men. Those who liked a soldier tended to rate him well across the board; disliked soldiers were rated consistently badly. Movie stars, politicians and business leaders rely heavily on the Halo Effect. If we think someone is attractive, we assume they're fascinating, talented and intelligent. Marketers use the Halo Effect for celebrity endorsements (if Brad Pitt buys it, it must be good). The only way to resist it is to think: is the headteacher on the podium really so fascinating, or is he just running a school you've heard good things about? Are the jeans flattering, or did they simply look good on Kate Moss? Is your boss really that clever, or has he simply Halo-Effected everyone on his way?

But hold on a second before you polish that halo of yours. You might have a sparkling reputation, but that of your team or organisation might not be so shiny. And just because you have a glowing reputation today doesn't mean that it won't all go belly-up tomorrow. Reputation has to be actively managed all of the time, not just when a crisis arises. But when one does crop up, know that you'll be judged on your attitude towards it – as well as the outcome.

Masterclass in Reputation Management: What is it?

Its advocates say reputation management is about so much more than mere spin. It involves preparing for sudden crises and scandals, dealing with investors, managing the brand and nurturing your firm's reputation, at once your most valuable and most delicate intangible asset. Reputations take years to establish but can be lost in an instant. Try not to get ahead of yourself, though. The old advice remains the best: don't lose your reputation before you've got one.

Where did it come from?

Just when it started looking as though boring old public relations was beginning to lose its mystique, some bright sparks in the industry pointed out that 'reputation management' could be packaged and sold as a more serious (and expensive) service. It blends in with high-powered 'corporate affairs' work – all that hush-hush stuff that goes on with regulators and government. But maybe it's just good old 'perception management' – which, of course, is public relations by any other name. So PR has done a good PR job on reputation management.

One of the best ways to manage your organisation's reputation is by uncovering any malpractice as quickly as possible. Instead of brushing problems under the carpet, foster an environment where wrongdoing is brought into the open and dealt with as quickly as possible. What if, for example, an audit has shown wrongdoing and financial irregularities that could cost your organisation dearly? Most worryingly, some staff knew what was going on but kept quiet. It's time your people were encouraged to blow the whistle…

CRASH COURSE IN...
WHISTLEBLOWING

Assess the risk. Your first step is to identify the risks the organisation faces in terms of wrongdoing and to assess the obstacles to people speaking out.

Broadcast the message. Explain to employees that they are encouraged to report malpractice and will not be penalised for doing so. Use a formal written whistleblowing policy to make clear what behaviours or practices are unacceptable – you may need to formulate standards and ethical policies.

Tell them who to tell. Create a three-tier hierarchy of disclosure. Whistleblowers should approach their own manager first; if no action is taken, they should inform a more senior manager. The third tier should be a board director or audit committee member who is concerned directly with the accountability of the organisation. An independent body should be proposed as a last resort.

It's not about grievances. If an employee's concern involves self-interest, handle it through a separate complaints procedure.

Protect the whistleblower. Most whistleblowers don't remain anonymous, but they may well expect their evidence to be treated in confidence. More to the point, the fundamental principle of the Public Interest Disclosure Act is that the whistleblower mustn't be victimised for coming forward. It's not just about them being sacked – there are plenty of other kinds of treatment that can end up leading to an employment tribunal. Some colleagues may resent their action, in which case you may have to consider moving the whistleblower to a different role.

Take it seriously. It's vital that you show a whistleblower that you take their claims seriously and are taking proper action. If they think you've done nothing, they might feel entitled to take it to a higher level or outside the organisation. If you do nothing, other whistleblowers will be discouraged from coming forward.

Guard against malice. Look out for 'disclosures' cooked up for malicious reasons. Investigate the claims thoroughly and make sure you give the other side a fair hearing. Don't go public if you don't need to. There's no inconsistency between encouraging your employees to report malpractice and asserting your contractual rights to keep people from passing sensitive information to the media.

Do say: 'If something wrong is happening in this organisation we need to know, so we can put it right.'

Don't say: 'We've got a special form for people wanting to snitch on their colleagues: it's called a P45.'

BRANDING

How your organisation's brand is perceived by your employees and the outside world is a good measure of your reputation. And a great brand can quickly translate into commercial success. It's critical therefore that you get your branding right, and more importantly, that you live up to the promises you make.

Masterclass in Branding:
What is it?

Everyone wants their goods and services to be memorable. That is what branding is all about. An effective brand conveys a distinctive message. It is both a label and an identity. It may well hint at the price at which you want to sell said goods and services. 'Brand equity' refers to the value contained within a brand. And the numbers here can be huge: up to half of the market capitalisation of companies such as Coca-Cola and McDonald's can be attributed to the value of the brand. No wonder companies worry so much about them.

Where did it come from?

Slave owners and livestock farmers have been branding for centuries. With the coming of mass production, business owners realised they needed to protect and promote the distinctive identity of their products. Modern branding had begun. In the 1930s, Neil McElroy, a marketing executive at Procter & Gamble, wrote a famous three-page memo that effectively invented the concept of 'brand management' (thereby launching a million careers). Marketing professionals were supposed to nurture and develop their brands and maintain their perceived value in the market so that a premium price could be charged. But brands are no longer simply about products: firms have an 'employer brand', and customers do not so much select certain brands as choose between 'customer experiences'. One thing is clear: marketers have rarely felt less in command of the work they do. Savvy ones now talk of 'co-creating' brands with the help of their customers – whatever that means.

WORDS-WORTH:
BRAND

'Brand' is an almost mystical idea that encompasses the whole character and reputation of a product or company. But it is a word with humble beginnings. In Anglo-Saxon times, a 'brand' was a piece of burning wood taken from the hearth. By the sixteenth century it had come to mean a mark made by burning with a hot iron. Animals were branded, to show ownership, but so were humans; the practice of branding criminals only became illegal in 1822. The first commercial use of the word came five years after that, in reference to a trade name burnt onto boxes. Later, the word spread from the mark to the thing marked: people began to ask for their 'usual brand'. Modern concepts of 'brand' were developed in the mid-twentieth century: that's when we first heard of 'brand loyalty', 'brand identity' and 'brand awareness'. When we talk about 'brand' now, we're often speaking of 'brand image', the impression a product creates in the minds of potential consumers; the idea was enthusiastically promoted in the late 1950s by the advertising giant David Ogilvy, and is now the responsibility of 'brand managers'. That's not a 'brand-new' title: the first were appointed in the US in the 1940s.

What if you think your organisation's brand is seriously lacking? The world has moved on, your use of design looks tired and the organisation itself is completely different from what it was five years ago. It's time to call in the brand doctors. But is it just about refreshing your logo, a change of name, or perhaps something more fundamental?

CRASH COURSE IN...
REBRANDING YOUR BUSINESS

Branding has moved on. It's the behaviours of your company and its people that form your reputation, and your reputation is your brand. What you're looking for is a simple idea – a brand essence or positioning – that expresses what the company is trying to do. Taglines, idents and the like will spring out of this.

Look in the mirror. You need to measure where you are at the moment, where you want to get to, and work out how you are going to bring it to life. What does your audience think of your corporate brand, and do they give you a licence to be what you want to become?

Take a reality check. It's important to balance aspiration and reality. If you say you're number one and you're not, you'll double the opprobrium you attract.

Pull back the curtains. The days when corporate branding strategy was dreamt up by three men in a darkened room are receding. Involve staff and they will buy into it; consult with stakeholders and they will tell you if you're off the rails. The days of unveiling a new branding in a Big Bang are pretty much dead. These days, it's a more gradual and pragmatic process.

Symbols are emotive. You can change the positioning of your brand without destroying the imagery people associate you with. However, refreshing your visual look to keep up with the times is a must every ten to fifteen years.

Orchestrate from the top. It needs to come from the leadership of the organisation, because they have to model the brand behaviours.

Ensure success. Make sure that the business strategy is well understood when your rebranding becomes public, and ensure that other aspects of communication such as advertising are consistent. Lastly, have the courage to continue with it if you know your brand is based on a fundamental truth and you have done your homework.

Do say: 'By articulating the values and behaviour that will make us a competitive success in the future, we can translate those into the elements of identity.'

Don't say: '"Maverick" has got a good ring to it.'

It might come as a surprise to some but the concept of branding can be applied to you as an individual – brand me. And there's a lot to be gained from it.

YOUR ROUTE TO THE TOP...
BE A WINNING BRAND

Specialise. Think like Google, Virgin and Coca-Cola – what do you want to be renowned for? Find your forte and focus on it.

Clarify your vision. What do you want to achieve with this brand? How can you align it with personal and career goals?

Live and breathe it. Don't try to be something you're not. Your brand is you. Just as a vegetarian doesn't eat meat when no one's looking, give it your all – all of the time.

Market yourself. What have you done today to let the world (or at least your colleagues and clients) know that you are uniquely contributing? Think about the best ways to advertise your message – network, create a website and LinkedIn profile, or write an industry blog.

Make your clients work for you. Assess their strengths: what can you actually learn from them? What do they say about you? Are they innovators? Do they add credibility to your brand? Your clients define you, so develop a future working strategy together.

Stay curious. Keep ahead of the competition by bringing a breadth of new experience to everything you do. Project stuck in a rut? Look through your contacts and find the most far removed person in there. Invite them out to lunch and pick their brains on what they would do.

Don't do things by halves. Starting with today's to-do list, do everything so that it makes you proud. If you can't get it right first time, postpone it until you can. Not happy with your client proposal? Reframe it as a draft to work on together rather than the final piece.

Keep it real. Don't leave your personality at home. Know the skills and traits that make you stand out from the rest. You are a whole package – so show people exactly what they get if they invest in you.

DIVERSITY

'Diversity' is a term that has become fashionable over the past few years. It's used to describe a policy that actively promotes the inclusion of anyone who isn't white and male. It's strange to think that a 'diversity' policy applies to 50 per cent of the population – women. But you shouldn't knock a good thing, and the sentiment behind diversity is honourable – to make sure that there is a diverse mix of people and therefore ideas, at every level of an organisation, including the upper echelons.

And it's not just about feeling good about doing the right thing (and portraying your organisation as an attractive and enlightened place to work); it's also about becoming more commercially successful. The latest business school research proves that the more diverse your senior management and boards are, the better you do. Not only does your reputation improve but your bottom line too. What's not to like?

So, you've always prided yourselves on being an Equal Opportunities organisation, but a visitor points out that your people look remarkably similar to each other. Are you discriminating against some groups without even knowing it? And could you be missing a trick? How do you achieve a truly diverse workforce?

CRASH COURSE IN...
DIVERSITY IN THE WORKPLACE

Comply or else. The need to comply with legislation is far from the only reason to take diversity seriously, but it's a good one. The employer now has to prove that they didn't discriminate, not the other way round.

Think opportunity. Diversity is about innovation and creativity. If you bring many different perspectives to a problem, you end up with more creative solutions. You want the best person for the job, full stop. So you want to recruit them from the widest possible pool. If you don't embrace diversity, you risk losing out.

Make your own business case. Look at how diversity could benefit your business directly. It could help you reach markets that aren't buying your products or services. Diversity shouldn't be about political correctness, it's about marketing and recognising changing demographics. Getting accreditation is also increasingly a requirement for procurement contracts.

Measure it. Data helps to identify where action is needed, and lets you demonstrate progress. If things are measured, they're taken seriously. You need to know not just who you recruit, but who applies, who is selected, promoted and so on.

Get out of your box. If your workforce or your customer base are under-represented, examine the root causes. Around 97 per cent of black and ethnic minority people don't read local newspapers, so if that's where you advertise when recruiting, you're missing out on 97 per cent of those communities.

Be holistic. Today, diversity is about race, gender, religion, sexual orientation, disability and age. Tomorrow, who knows? It could be about fat and thin or even beautiful and ugly. The important thing is to keep an open mind and to value people as individuals.

Share responsibility. Diversity needs support at the top, and it must be embraced throughout the organisation. Your top team must give permission to take the agenda forward, but while you may designate one person with ultimate responsibility, they need to be an engine-room for change, rather than someone the issue gets dumped on. Training will help your people understand the benefits of diversity.

Do say: 'We think that people's differences make us stronger.'

Don't say: 'I've got nothing against gays, blacks or anyone else. They just never seem to apply for a job here.'

Unfortunately, some glass ceilings are tougher to crack than others …

History lessons: Joan of Arc

Women trying to break into the top echelons of business might take heart from the example of Joan of Arc. At just sixteen, her premonitory visions of future military victories won her one of the most challenging management positions available in the early 1400s: commander of the massed French armies in their war against the English. She donned her outsized armour and took to battle with a religious zeal. But it was only after she pulled an arrow from her shoulder in the heat of battle that her macho commanders took her seriously, acknowledging that unlike the other women they knew, this one had balls. Joan lived by men's rules but also died by them. She was eventually abandoned to the Burgundians, sold to the English and (illegally) burnt at the stake. Business women in the twenty-first century may prefer not to take things so far. Admire Joan for her macho spirit, but live and work by your own rules. Martyrdom just isn't worth it.

You've got loads of women in the organisation. So why aren't they reaching the top, and what can you do?

CRASH COURSE IN...
DISMANTLING THE GLASS CEILING

Get the basics in place. Your starting point should be an equal opportunities policy, making it clear that discrimination will not be operated or allowed. Everyone needs to be made aware of the policy and to understand that those who don't abide by it will be disciplined.

Cater for lifestyle needs. Flexible working and childcare support – e.g., through a workplace crèche – aren't beneficial just to women; but without them many will struggle to fly as high as they could. It's not just about giving women (and men) the opportunity to work flexibly, it's ensuring that they're not seen as less committed and generally second-class citizens.

Monitor the situation. Some organisations carry out detailed pipeline analysis of potential women leaders throughout the organisation. We now have more understanding of the dynamics of our work population. They can then assess where the hotspots or blockages are, and formulate action plans.

Analyse career paths. Research has found job segregation to be a significant factor in career advancement, with a perception that many organisations draw senior appointments from male-dominated disciplines. Companies should review procedures and ensure they're finding the best talent wherever it is – e.g., by looking at softer areas such as HR. Getting the right all-round experience is key for women. Many would like international know-how.

Coach for self-confidence. Self-confidence is a big issue for many women, because they often feel they haven't had a linear career and they're more likely to have moved sideways. Coaching can boost self-confidence. Mentoring can also help open doors for women with potential.

Foster a less macho culture. Try replacing the office outings to Spearmint Rhino and awaydays on TA exercises with cultural activities. Hey presto, you may find more talented women attracted to your portals.

Consider special measures. Some organisations have designed a women's leadership programme to provide a positive intervention and address the imbalance at the top. But…

Use quotas at your peril. Positive discrimination in appointments or filling quotas at certain levels helps to provide the role models needed but it undermines credibility – people will say you're only there because it was a female shortlist.

Do say: 'What really makes the best person for this job?'

Don't say: 'You must be the new secretary.'

DO THE RIGHT THING

Genuinely brilliant leaders will want to do the right thing. This doesn't mean dragging your staff to a monastic retreat once a month but it does mean instilling a sense of morality into the very heart of your organisation. With current levels of cynicism towards the private sector running high, being admired for the way you do business will enhance your reputation for being a trusted organisation – a priceless quality to possess.

Masterclass in Morality in Business: What is it?

Suddenly, everybody wants to (re)discover their moral core. As a reaction to the financial crisis and the near-death experiences of recession, some business leaders have started speaking up about the need to improve ethical standards. Bankers were derided for their 'socially useless' activity, while politicians from all parties call for tougher regulation and an end to the bonus culture. But the most moral task facing managers is to try to keep their commercial show on the road. There may have to be a trade-off between what is right and what is necessary.

Where did it come from?

There have always been critics who have found capitalism too raw for their taste. During the English Civil War, the Levellers argued for greater equality and less corruption in public life. In the nineteenth century, Karl Marx and Friedrich Engels developed their critique that changed the course of history. And John Ruskin, the art critic, wrote his treatise *Unto This Last*, which championed the cause of restraint for the rich and social justice for the poor. But while the protests continued, so did trade, and business empires created enormous wealth around the world – for some. And now, how many City dignitaries have actually committed themselves to doing things differently? Cynics question whether there can be greater morality in business when there are deals to be done and competitors to be beaten…

Doing right by our planet is another major concern for a leader worth their salt. Any future business progress must be sustainable – but going green doesn't mean forfeiting valuable profits. Every leader's concern right now will and should be focused on pulling out of recession and concentrating on future profits but becoming a sustainable organisation will help you get there.

WORDS-WORTH:
GREEN

These days, most businesses profess to be 'green', meaning 'conscious of the environment'. Old English green symbolises jealousy. To be green is to be fresh and youthful, but also immature, gullible and naive. The environmental sense came from German left-wing politics, starting with Grüne Aktion Zukunft *(Green Action for the Future) in 1969. At the same time in Canada, some young draft-dodgers, hippies and radicals started a group to oppose the Vietnam War and nuclear testing. They wanted to call it the Green Panthers, but someone came up with the slogan 'Make it a green peace' and they used that instead. In 1985, the Ecology Party in Britain decided its name was too 'middle-class' and opted for the Green Party. Three years later, the first* Green Consumer Guide *was published. Where there were consumers, producers and retailers had to follow. The expression 'green business' was first heard in the early 1990s. The arrival of the biodegradable Tesco bag took a little longer.*

You may used to have thought that being green was a luxury for your company, but climate change has made you realise that you can no longer ignore it. The buzz is about becoming carbon-neutral, but where do you start?

CRASH COURSE IN...
BECOMING CARBON-NEUTRAL

Consider your drivers. Do you want to become carbon-neutral for marketing reasons, for financial reasons, or just to save the planet? Your drivers will help to tailor your carbon-reduction programme and determine key performance indicators. Build a case for going carbon-neutral.

Measure it. First, measure your current carbon footprint – or get a specialist to do it for you. That primarily means taking account of your energy usage and emissions caused through travel. Before you begin, think about whether you're collecting the right data and whether it's readily accessible.

Switch it off. Most companies can save around 15–20 per cent of their energy consumption through a combination of measures such as getting people to turn off lights, resetting temperature switches, reducing air-conditioning use and insulating.

Stay put. Look at cutting out non-essential air and road travel, and create a policy on when staff should travel. A state-of-the-art video-conferencing facility could obviate the need for many trips. And look at introducing more efficient vehicles into your fleet.

Engage your people. It's much better if your people decide for themselves when it's sensible for them to travel. You'll also need them to participate in switching off the lights and other energy-saving measures. Explain how it will benefit the business – as well as the planet – by saving costs. Do you really need an office in Paris that produces no revenue? And would bringing services back in-house be more energy-efficient? Becoming a low- or no-carbon firm aids recruitment and retention.

Make demands of your suppliers. Think about differentiating yourself by offering low-carbon products. Work with your supply partners to find ways of reducing the carbon content.

Offset with care. You can wipe out the impact of your energy use at a stroke by switching to renewables. Then offset your residual carbon impact by investing in projects in the developing world – where your money goes further – that will reduce global carbon emissions. But make sure the offsets you purchase are independently verified.

Set targets. It's not a one-off exercise. Next year, you can save even more energy. You'll also save more money, spend less on offsets, and your financial director will be a happy bunny.

Do say: 'Our aim is to minimise our own carbon impacts, to work with suppliers and customers to help them do the same, and to invest in measures that will cancel out our contribution to climate change.'

Don't say: 'Climate change is going to present us with some exciting new marketing opportunities.'

SUCCESSION

'The legacy of heroes is the memory of a great name and the inheritance of a great example'
BENJAMIN DISRAELI SAID IT

Though you may still be in your early days as a leader, it's never too soon to think about what kind of legacy you want to leave. This means considering such things as succession planning and grooming those in the team around you that you think might be able to pick up the baton.

Masterclass in Succession Planning: What is it?

The graveyards are filled with indispensable men, it is sometimes said. Even if the remark is ironic, it reminds us that leaders and managers who are here today may be gone tomorrow – to a rival business, into retirement, or to the great meeting-room in the sky. Sensible businesses plan for these eventualities. They maintain a 'pipeline of talent'. Younger managers ('high potentials') can be given stretching assignments to speed up their development and help them acquire experience. They'll then be better prepared when gaps appear. What could go wrong?

Where did it come from?

In the good old days, we had careers. We worked for businesses that could be represented on organisational charts. Life seemed predictable. When management thinker Charles Handy was a junior manager at Shell, he was told what he would be doing, where and when, over the next thirty years. Handy eventually ran away, appalled (bet the succession plan at Shell hadn't allowed for that). But, gradually, time-serving started to lose some of its power as a qualification for promotion. Ageism emerged too, and with it the idea that some jobs were really 'a young person's game'. Careers got shorter, and succession plans were torn up. Now, firms tend to follow a twin-track policy on succession planning. Key employees – 'talent' – are nurtured. These are the people in pivotal positions who you really don't want to lose. The rest? Well... good luck to them. But the employee can have the last laugh here.

Aided by online social networks, people can tout themselves to future employers. They can create their own succession plan. After all, employers have been telling them for some time that there is 'no job for life any more'. Now you too can be a person with a plan.

In the war for talent, identifying and nurturing the bright young things under your nose is not just a strategic manoeuvre, it's your lifeblood. Fail in this and your most promising people will achieve their potential elsewhere, leaving you with a vacuum at the top of your organisation. But where to start?

CRASH COURSE IN...
DEVELOPING FUTURE LEADERS

Do it once a year. Most big companies operate an annual talent review as part of the planning cycle. It takes time to get people ready to take on the big roles, so if you're looking for a senior manager to be appointed in two years' time, you need to be working on them now.

Bring on the scouts. Line managers are the best-placed people to spot talent. Historically, HR has tried to own the process, but the guys at the edge of the pitch are the best placed to identify tomorrow's stars. Nevertheless, line managers need to be acutely aware that they don't own the talent in their department – the organisation does.

Identify the X-factors. Current performance doesn't always predict future potential – today's high performers are not always tomorrow's stars. Success in their current role may be a prerequisite for fast-tracking someone, but additional qualities are usually sought. Look for judgement, drive and an ability to influence others. Identify people who are good at learning, can master complexity, want to lead, and who balance passion for results with their values.

Look to the future. Don't assess high potentials for what you need now or what has worked in the past – think about the business's future needs. IBM used to make computers, now it's all about services.

Evaluate your assets. Once you've conducted your trawl, establish just how good the chosen few really are. Role-playing, psychometric tests and 360-degree appraisals are often used. It's a detailed diagnosis of where the gaps are between where the person is now and where you want them to be in a couple of years' time.

Fast forward. The next job is to create an accelerated development plan that brings them up to speed in the required areas. They'll need extensive support.

Keep it open. If the process is secretive, people will think it's unfair. You don't have to broadcast every line manager's recommendations, but make your talent management policy transparent.

Don't write anyone off. It's largely a question of readiness. Some high-flyers are just a bit slower to take off.

Do say: 'We want to give our brightest and best every chance to lead this organisation in the future.'

Don't say: 'Anyone who's any good will get to the top eventually, anyway. They don't need us to help them.'

If you haven't already established a formal (or informal) mentoring scheme, then it is something that you should seriously consider.

Masterclass in Mentoring:
What is it?

A mentor is a senior colleague or acquaintance who provides continuous advice to a more junior person. Mentoring is not the same as coaching. The 'mentee' may have a greater emotional investment in the relationship than should be the case with a coach, and the mentor is not as dispassionate as a coach should be. Mentoring allows an inexperienced manager to benefit from someone with a more seasoned perspective. The mentor may act as a sounding board or as an inspirational role model and may play devil's advocate or simply teach valuable lessons.

Where did it come from?

In Greek mythology, Mentor was Odysseus's trusted adviser and friend. In due course, Athena (the goddess of wisdom, not the poster shop) took the form of Mentor and appeared before the wanderer's son Telemachus, also acting as a guide. It has always been a smart career move to latch on to someone at or near the top, and try and draw on their experience (and contacts). Alternatively, staying in touch with a 'retired' person can be beneficial. Just because the corporate memory has been outsourced or let go doesn't mean it should be ignored. Nearly three-quarters of UK organisations use mentoring schemes. Most plan to increase their use of mentoring over the next few years. Mentoring isn't easy; it requires the time and commitment of both parties. But it may be one of the best ways to advance your career or break through the glass ceiling. There's no need for female mentors to disguise themselves any more.

LESSONS FROM THE TOP

That's enough of the theory; it's time to get some advice from the horse's mouth. As every leader will admit, it's one thing to imagine yourself in the hot seat but quite another to actually be sitting in it.

What follows is some of the best leadership and career advice from the top movers and shakers in the UK. Respected leaders in their fields, here they open up and spill the beans on the secrets to their success. What does it mean to be a leader, whether chief executive, politician or chairman?

IN THEIR OWN WORDS...

Archie Norman, chairman, ITV

'[On becoming Asda's CEO in 1991] I walked in the door of a bankrupt organisation that employed 60,000 people. They were all waiting for a new chief executive and it was me – and that was one of those traumatic moments, when every tiny step is disproportionately important. Those early years were good because we were very much a team and we had a common mission: to survive. They were tough but we didn't know anything else. We never realised what a good business we had. That's a profound point. The pace of success meant we never sat back and looked at how far we'd come or what we'd achieved.'

SIR JOHN HARVEY-JONES
LATE CHAIRMAN OF ICI

'You have to give your people headroom and power and really trust them. The first thing I did after halving the size of the board [at ICI] was to cut out the controls. We used twenty-one key performance indicators – worse than the bloody government. My aim the whole time was to increase the number of people who could say yes and decrease the number of people who could say no. It didn't matter so much if they were right or wrong, so long as they did something and did it fast.'

Lord Myners, former chair of M&S, Land Securities Group and the Guardian Media Group

'The chairman shouldn't interfere in the day-to-day management of the business. He should be a mentor to the chief executive. He should be available for conversations the chief executive can't easily hold with other people in the company. All chief executives, however good they are, have moments of doubt as well as inspiration, and the chairman should be available for those.'

Chris Hyman, CEO, Serco

'Nothing keeps change going more than both the heart and head being motivated by that change. You need to inspire through oratory but you also need to be fixed on a goal, such as a bonus if you succeed... I'm in this office about four days a month. The rest of the time, I'm out. I do 100 flights a year. I see 200 staff at a time. No managers or directors are allowed.

It's just me and them. They can tell me what they want, about anything. I've also got "tellchris.com", where they can e-mail me any concerns. I also hold regular dinners – the rule is they're for ten people in the company I've never met. My staff have my mobile phone number but they don't contact me very often; when they do, they feel strongly about it – it's a big deal to phone the boss. But if we don't get it right, I deserve the calls. When they do, I meet them. I never reply straight on e-mail. I want to see the person, see the whites of their eyes. It makes a huge difference, seeing the whites of someone's eyes – it can really move me.'

PHILIP YEA
FORMER CEO, 3i GROUP

'The job of any CEO is to earn shareholders' trust. One of the challenges is the belief that everything is analysable. I got asked recently by a potential investor to explain the leverage multiples of the deals we did at the beginning of the year versus those we did at the end. I said: "Look, this information will not help you." There comes a point where analysis stops, where what you have to do is believe in your people, their experience and in the systems and processes you have for making decisions. If you tried to analyse everything you would go mad.'

James Murdoch, CEO, News Corporation

'You read about Sky being in a bunch of mud huts out in Osterley – that's what they think in Soho – but we like having all our operations in one place. It's better to be a bit separate and it allows us to forge a challenger culture which we nourish… At our worst, we slow down and start to think we're established. That's when we are vulnerable.'

Michael Grade, former chairman of the BBC and former CEO of ITV

'I've never planned my career. I've always worked on the basis that you do whatever job you do and you do it to the best of your ability. New opportunities open up. My world turned upside-down really with the move to the BBC [he was brought in as chairman in 2004]. That was kind of coming back to the media, which I never expected to do. It was a huge change for me, and that was kind of a seminal moment.'

JOHN VARLEY
CEO, BARCLAYS

'In the last twenty-four hours I rang a customer who'd been having a problem with us that wasn't his fault. Saying sorry always helps. And I've visited a customer who has been with us for a long time – both with his business and his personal affairs. I went to see if we could do more for him. Visits like that are why I'm in this business. If things have gone wrong, putting them right can be fulfilling.'

Kim Winser, former CEO of Aquascutum and Pringle

'Be enthusiastic, passionate, come up with ideas, implement them, move forward. If you're in the job or profession that is right for you, that you care about, then you'll shine … One of the most exciting things for me is to get the best out of people. I don't expect anybody to be the same. I don't employ clones. I like people to have their own complete personalities – I love that – but so long as they achieve the most they can with support, with resource, with direction, with enthusiasm, then I feel really rewarded.'

LORD COE
CHAIRMAN, LONDON ORGANISING COMMITTEE FOR THE OLYMPIC GAMES

'**I've never planned anything in my career.** I'm not one of those who says: at twenty-four I'll be doing this, at thirty I'll be an MP, at forty I'll be in the Cabinet or else I'll be a failure. My life has been a series of blocks, like the Olympics every four years. In 1980, in Moscow, I walked off the track – I couldn't tell you what I was doing next. I lived in Italy for two years and taught and tried for 1984, in LA. I went and sat on a beach in Malibu and thought about what I should do. I'd always been interested in politics, so I thought I'd get into front-line politics.'

Vince Cable MP, Business Secretary

'One thing that really impressed me [about working at Shell as chief economist], and that I have desperately tried to communicate in politics, was the way Shell let go of its operating companies and allowed them to do their own thing. Big companies understand that you can't run everything out of one central office, but that's the way Gordon Brown tried to run the country. It's completely mad.'

JOANNA SHIELDS
VICE PRESIDENT, FACEBOOK

'I love [deal making] but I have this philosophy. Every deal should have a balance. Imbalance is what creates the tension in the future, and when you're trying to create a partnership that is long term and sustaining you can't take the last dollar or pound from the table. You have to have fairness. In the long run, it serves a purpose because people feel they got the value. Then they are loyal and they feel good and they continue to work with you.'

Willie Walsh, CEO, British Airways

'Good opportunities don't come up very often, and when they do you've got to take them. I tend to be the kind of guy who says yes and then thinks about it afterwards. I think I've got most of those calls right.'

Mike Lynch, CEO, Autonomy

'The most important thing I was ever taught was the idea of focus. The way it was put to me was: take the one hundred things that you think you're supposed to be doing, put them in order of importance and then only do the top five. The rest don't really matter.'

Stevie Smith, CEO, Future

'The essence of good leadership should be the same in the good times as the bad times. You can be a bad leader in good times and still get results because of the marketplace, but in bad times, a bad leader gets found out. You have to lead by example – what you do is as important as what you say. It's less of an act and more an absolute belief.'

Rosaleen Blair, CEO, Alexander Mann Solutions

'One of the things that is quite damaging is the view that women can have it all. That puts an enormous strain and challenge on young women, because they feel that they are going to have to make choices, and I don't think that's true. You can have it all, but it needs to be at different stages in your life and your career. It's about life balance, as opposed to work/life balance.'

IF I HAD TO START AGAIN...

You can learn a lot from leaders who have gone before you. What would some of the UK's top leaders do differently if they could start all over again? Here's some career advice with the benefit of hindsight from the very top...

SIR ROCCO FORTE
FOUNDER OF RF HOTELS

'I grew up in an environment where my father was immersed in his business, and my overriding impression to this day is of him at work or of accompanying him on visits to hotels and restaurants. My father's passion for his work influenced me to such a degree that anything that delayed my going into the business seemed an impediment. My time at Oxford was great fun, as were my three years of accounting, but both delayed the day I could start real work. Within Forte my progress was rapid but I was protected by my father from the real rigours of business life. I did not have to make the most serious decisions until my last few years there. I have since put my knowledge and experience to good use in developing my own luxury hotels company, RF Hotels, which I can drive exactly as I please. So, if I were to live my life again, I would make sure that, early on, I worked in an organisation where I was on my own and where I had to earn my own spurs. Even so, it taught me the importance of hard work, gave me a passion for my industry and a belief in customer service.'

SIR JEREMY ISAACS
FOUNDING CHIEF EXECUTIVE OF
CHANNEL 4

'It may have been natural to become an MP. I enjoyed being involved in politics at Oxford and, having studied Classics, I had no idea what else to do. The general secretary of the Labour Party in Scotland put me right: five tough questions demonstrated that I knew absolutely nothing about anything. But I had enjoyed being present when figures like Nye Bevan and Clement Attlee spoke, so I thought of a job in TV. In 1958 I was hired as a researcher by Granada where, among other things, I wrote the weather forecast. I mentioned anti-cyclones and was told: "We don't use words like that here, it's either wet or dry." I thought that was marvellous – it didn't matter that you could translate a line or two of Homer; what mattered was that you could communicate. I quickly realised I wanted to use the medium to explain the world to people. After only eighteen months at Granada I was producing *What the Papers Say*. I am hugely proud of *The World at War*, but when I say I "made" it, the truth is it took fifty people three years to make. The most exciting and difficult thing I ever had to do was get Channel 4 off the ground. We started with an almost blank piece of paper, and we had an absolute whale of a time doing things no one had done before.'

Sir Christopher Bland, former chairman of BT

'I had a desire to be a journalist, but I paid no attention at university to what I needed for such a career. When I left Oxford after studying modern history, the BBC quite rightly wouldn't interview me. I'd been a burden to my parents for twenty-two years and simply wanted a job, so ended up as an assistant ad manager at Currys. I was paid £1,000 a year, which was generous back then – Shell paid £800. I had no guiding philosophy, and my career was pretty random. I went from Currys to Singer, then to Booz Allen Hamilton as a management consultant. But I'd always wanted to be a hands-on chief executive, so I took that role at locomotive builder Beyer Peacock in 1975. They were tiny – the market cap was equivalent to a day's interest on BT's bank borrowings when I arrived. I've been fortunate to have had five great jobs, as chairman of Hammersmith Hospital Trust, the BBC, BT, the RSC and LWT. For five months, I chaired both the BBC and BT – both national institutions, very much in the public eye. It's important to enjoy what you're doing. There's no point just plugging away at something just to pull in a wage. Otherwise, what are we all doing here? Business is like falling in love – you don't know the right thing until you find it.'

GENERAL SIR MICHAEL JACKSON
THE BRITISH ARMY'S FORMER CHIEF OF THE GENERAL STAFF

'**I wouldn't swap my army life for anything.** Operational command was the most rewarding thing I've experienced, and I ended on quite an adventure – Kosovo in 1999. As a commander in the field, your responsibility is absolute: getting it right gives a great sense of achievement, but it involves risk, and there have been times when, very sadly, I've had to bury friends. I was, for example, very close to Warrenpoint, location of the deadly attack by the IRA on August bank holiday, 1979. They murdered Mountbatten in the morning, then had a go at the British Army in the afternoon. Eighteen soldiers were killed. That's the hard part, but it is, of course, the nature of the game. Your life depends on your mate, and vice versa. My father, who fought in the Second World War, was clearly an influence on me. I'd always wanted to go to Sandhurst, and did when I was eighteen. My youngest son has just passed his initial selection there too. I tell him he must be clear about it in his own mind, and not just follow Dad. It's an important decision for a young person, how they see their life unfolding. I just urge him to enjoy it hugely – to the best of my knowledge, you're only here once.'

Lord Puttnam, film producer

'I'd throw myself into the digital world with the same self-belief I had entering the ad industry in the 1960s. I had loathed school and left with no qualifications, and replied to an ad for a messenger boy at the *Evening Standard*. I loved work, and was soon at an [advertising] agency alongside Alan Parker, Ridley Scott and Charles Saatchi. There was a lot of laughter, and a real sense the world was changing and you could do anything. At twenty-eight, through a mix of ludicrous arrogance and complete lack of knowledge, I got into the film industry. For the first time, I felt like a round peg in a round hole. My first production was well received. But I learnt more from producing my second film, Jacques Demy's *Pied Piper*, which starred Donovan and was catastrophic. I had a hit with *Midnight Express* in 1977. It paid off my overdraft, but it wasn't how I wanted to work, and out of that experience came my more personal films: *Chariots of Fire*, *Local Hero* and *The Killing Fields*. In 1986 I took a job heading Columbia Pictures. It was an honest mistake. The nature of the deal guaranteed me an income, the fruits of which I still live on. But was I happy? No. Was I suited to the job? No. It was like being a general in the Second World War, up in the château poring over maps when you're best out commanding the troops. I quit film in 1998.'

LORD LAMONT
FORMER CHANCELLOR OF THE EXCHEQUER

'**I would like to try something different, so I might be a barrister.** Miscarriages of justice make me angry, and it would be satisfying to stand up for people against the whims of fashion and public opinion. Also, I think the life at the Bar is a nice one. I like the independence: you're self-employed and – unlike politics – answerable only to your client. In business, it's perfectly all right to suddenly decide to pursue a totally different strategy; in politics, you can't do that. And businesspeople have to make decisions quickly, based on the best available information. In politics, there is an endless quest for perfection, for more information to precisely calibrate every decision. I think many business people can't see the point. My favourite job as a politician was Chancellor of the Exchequer. There's nothing a government can do without the assent of the Treasury, including go to war. It's very rewarding, and I say that even though I had a rough time. I didn't want to be PM though – being PM is like being chairman of a company which holds a shareholders' meeting every week, and a pretty angry one at that. I wouldn't have chosen to come out of the European Exchange Rate Mechanism [on Black Wednesday, 16 September 1992] in the way we did, but I don't really see how the decisions we made could have been different – the facts drove them. However, the ERM did cure Britain's inflation problem, and after it had done that it disintegrated. It made me look a little ridiculous, but what does that matter? One thing I'd do differently is to speak more plainly and not tell any jokes. When I said *"je ne regrette rien"*, it was a frivolous answer to a frivolous question. It doesn't mean you aren't very serious.'

Greg Dyke, former Director-General of the BBC

'We'd all love to have been professional footballers or concert pianists, but we have to work with the talent we've got. For me, that was about working out strategies, running things and motivating people. I went into TV at thirty, after a spell as a journalist and a stint at Wandsworth Council, and I ended up with the top job as Director-General of the BBC. I'm proud that I did it without compromising my values. If I could go back in time I'd still take the BBC job. There are things we'd all do differently, but on the major issues by and large I think I got it right. I do, however, regret the way it ended. When I was writing my autobiography, my wife said: "Why do you never leave anywhere like anyone else?" And I suppose she's right; when I join or leave a company it's usually controversial. That must be something about me. I don't spend enough time thinking about the way I was treated to feel aggrieved about it. That said, if the opportunity ever came for revenge against a few people I would certainly take it, and every so often it does. When I look back to the Hutton Inquiry, [the inquiry into the BBC's reporting of Dr David Kelly's findings on Iraq's weapons of mass destruction] I said there were quite a lot of gutless people around and I still feel the same way. I don't meet many people who don't believe that they [the Blair government and its advisers] sexed up that dossier and the case for war. So it's a shame it happened, because I was enjoying the job and I still felt there was more to be done – but that's life. Living through the good times is easy; it's about living through the tough times and how you react to them that's the real test.'

LORD BROWNE
FORMER CEO OF BP

'I would do many things exactly the same. The reason I went into business was because my father pushed me with a very simple question: "Why not try it?" I did. And I loved it – I loved the oil industry and the richness of all the experiences I had and the people I met. The one thing I would change is the way I handled the situation that ultimately resulted in my departure from BP. I made one fatal error of judgement when I told an untruth in a document given to the High Court about how my ex-partner Jeff Chevalier and I met. It was a very bad thing to have done – something I had never done before and I'm confident I would never do again. I corrected the statement and apologised, but by then it was too late. If I were doing it all again, I would like [my sexuality] to be very transparent. But it was unrealistic at that time – it was very difficult to bring my two lives together. Things were quite different when I was growing up from how they are today; unless you were in a highly sophisticated minority, you weren't out. And in corporate life then it was basically unacceptable to be out, and the fact it was the oil industry just made it tougher. In retrospect, I may have stayed on too long at BP.

It's always difficult to judge when you should go. It's probably the most difficult thing for leaders to do. There's always more to be done – there's always another problem to be solved; but in the end it's a fallacy, because life is continuous for a corporation like BP, as it should be. The best thing you can do is to help develop great people to take over from you.'

Rod Aldridge, founder, Capita

'As a child, I had a great home life, but I didn't have the tools to be as good as I felt I should be academically. And that's quite frustrating. But if you've got determination, you find other routes. One of mine was sport – I was good at football and cricket. I was also very good at dance. I competed in modern sequence dancing from the age of eight to nineteen – I even danced at the Royal Albert Hall. That gave me the supreme confidence I was good at something: it showed me that I had the ability to do something others admire. It wasn't easy leaving Capita – it almost meant too much to me to let it go. A lot of entrepreneurs struggle to get the timing right as to when they leave the business, but I was in danger of staying longer than was right for me. The circumstances around my departure weren't very pleasant. [Aldridge resigned as chairman of Capita after it was revealed that he had lent the Labour Party £1m. The accusation, strongly denied by the company, was that Capita secured government contracts as a result.]

As far as I was concerned, I had made a personal decision, but I was caught up in a much bigger story. I certainly don't feel aggrieved by what happened. It would have been far worse to have left a business if I'd fallen out with long-term colleagues, or if I'd underperformed for shareholders. I did neither. The excitement of starting a business and seeing it grow – particularly the way Capita did – is phenomenal.'

AND FINALLY...

This book serves as a manual to keep within easy reach as you learn the leadership ropes. But as the great American business guru Henry Mintzberg said: 'Leadership, like swimming, cannot be learnt by reading about it.' You have to get out there and start being the leader you want to be. Good luck, and know that you have help and inspiration to hand...

MORE TO
EXPLORE

BIBLIOGRAPHY

Chris Anderson (2006), *The Long Tail*, Random House

Chris Anderson (2009), *Free*, Random House

Paul Arden (2006), *Whatever You Think, Think the Opposite*,
Penguin

Sally Bibb & Jeremy Kourdi (2007), *A Question of Trust*,
Marshall Cavendish

John Browne (2010), *Beyond Business*, Weidenfeld &
Nicolson

Todd G. Buchholz (2007), *New Ideas from Dead CEOs*,
Collins

Business Essential (2009), A&C Black

Clayton Christensen (1997), *The Innovator's Dilemma*,
Harvard Business Press

Clayton Christensen (2003), *The Innovator's Solution*,
Harvard Business Press

Jim Collins (2001), *Good to Great*, Random House

Jim Collins (2006), *Good to Great and the Social Sector*,
Random House

Jim Collins (2009), *How the Mighty Fall*, Random House

Stephen R. Covey (2004), *The Seven Habits of Highly
Effective People*, new edition, Simon & Schuster

Stephen R. Covey with Rebecca R. Merrill (2006),
The Speed of Trust, Simon & Schuster

Carly Fiorina (2006), *Tough Choices*, Nicholas Brealey

Stewart D. Friedman (2008), *Total Leadership*, Harvard Business Press

Howard Gardner, (2006), *Five Minds for the Future*, Harvard Business Press

Emmanuel Gobillot (2009), *Leadershift*, Kogan Page

Rob Goffee & Gareth Jones (2006), *Why Should Anyone Be Led by You?*, Harvard Business Press

Marshall Goldsmith (2009), *Succession*, Harvard Business Press

Charles Handy (2007), *Myself and Other More Important Matters*, Arrow

Jeff Howe (2009), *Crowdsourcing*, Random House

Leander Kahney (2009), *Inside Steve's Brain*, Atlantic Books

Allan Leighton (2007), *On Leadership*, Random House

Jerry Porras & Jim Collins (2002), *Built to Last*, Harper

Gary Marcus (2008), *Kluge*, Faber and Faber

The Mind Gym (2005), *Wake Up Your Mind*, Sphere

The Mind Gym (2006), *Give Me Time*, Time Warner Books

The Mind Gym (2009), *Relationships*, Sphere

Jo Owen (2007), *Power at Work*, Prentice Hall Business

Tom Peters & Robert H. Waterman (2004), *In Search of Excellence*, new edition, Profile Business

Richard Reeves & John Knell (2009), *The 80 Minute MBA*, Headline Business Plus

Phil Rosenzweig (2007), *The Halo Effect*, Simon & Schuster

Alan Ruddock (2007), *Michael O'Leary*, Penguin

Alice Schroeder (2008), *The Snowball*, Bloomsbury

Steve Tappin and Andrew Cave (2008), *The Secrets of CEOs*, Nicholas Brealey Publishing

Don Tapscott & Anthony D. Williams (2007), *Wikinomics*, Atlantic Books

Peninah Thomson and Jacey Graham (with Tom Lloyd), 2008, *A Woman's Place is in the Boardroom*, Palgrave Macmillan

Andrew Wileman (2010), *Driving Down Cost*, new edition, Nicholas Brealey Publishing

Avivah Wittenburg-Cox & Alison Maitland (2009), *Why Women Mean Business*, John Wiley & Sons

PICTURE CREDITS

We would like to thank the following for kindly supplying material for use in this book:

Getty Images – pp. 24, 69
iStock – pp. 38, 53, 62, 74, 81, 89, 94, 109, 128
Patrick Regout – pp. 28, 57, 91, 102, 112, 116, 126

INDEX

Note: Page numbers in bold denote major sections.

THE MANAGEMENT MASTERCLASS

Great business ideas without the hype

Emma De Vita

'Sensible management advice that's actually comprehensible and even occasionally witty.'

Robert Peston, BBC Business Editor

Imagine you could come up with winning solutions to prickly business issues on a regular basis. Where would the inspiration come from? Welcome to *The Management Masterclass*.

There are five sections to get your teeth into, which cover the personal values and skills needed to be a brilliant manager, how to create a happy team that will go the extra mile, the all-important financials, common challenges and how to best deal with them and finally the low-down on getting ahead and standing out from the crowd.

The Management Masterclass gives you practical, no-nonsense advice, delivered in a way that will help you climb the greasy pole, support others as you ascend and have fun on the way up.

If you want to keep your finger on the pulse of the most up-to-date business practice around, you need to read *The Management Masterclass*.

Non-fiction/Business 978 0 7553 6014 7

headline
business plus

More exciting titles from Business Plus

Know Me, Like Me, Follow Me
Penny Power and Thomas Power   £9.99

A guide to understanding the online environment from an expert author who created Ecademy, the world's first online business network.

The King of Shaves Story
Will King   £9.99

Will King hand-filled the first 10,000 bottles of his original shaving oil at his kitchen sink! King of Shaves has since grown to become a multi-million pound business. Will explains how to keep the faith and follow your business dream even when the odds are stacked against you.

The Secret Laws of Management
Stuart Wyatt   £10.99

Stuart Wyatt distils the essence of great business into 40 succinct and memorable laws. These laws will quickly become guiding principles that you can follow, and use to avoid the pitfalls into which others fall. The solutions are helpful, intelligent and often surprising.

Enduring Success
Sir Steve Redgrave   £12.99

An inspiring analysis of success that will help business readers understand how long-term success is achieved. During his sporting career, which spans nearly a quarter of a century,

Steve learned to face the challenges of redefining goals, learning new skills, fighting off renewed competition, making difficult choices and staying motivated.

The Management Masterclass
Emma De Vita   £10.99

Emma De Vita gives practical, no-nonsense advice, delivered in a way that will help you climb the greasy pole, help others as you ascend and have fun on the way up. If you want to keep your finger on the pulse of the most up-to-date business practice, you need to read this book.

What's Your Bright Idea?
Tim Campbell and Paul Humphries   £10.99

Starting your own business can be the most liberating, fulfilling step you've ever taken but you need a trusted guide, particularly in the tricky early stages. This inspirational guide gives the reader practical advice and bucket loads of enthusiasm in equal measure.

To order, simply call 01235 400 414 or email
orders@bookpoint.co.uk

FREE P&P AND DELIVERY
(Overseas and in Ireland add £3.50 per book)

Prices and availability are subject to change without notice.